# In Sickness and In Health

# In Sickness and In Health

*A Journalized Account of Coping
with Multiple Myeloma*

## Demetria Alexander Grissett

authorHOUSE®

*AuthorHouse™*
*1663 Liberty Drive*
*Bloomington, IN 47403*
*www.authorhouse.com*
*Phone: 1-800-839-8640*

*Published by AuthorHouse    08/24/2012*

*ISBN: 978-1-4772-6341-9 (sc)*
*ISBN: 978-1-4772-6340-2 (hc)*
*ISBN: 978-1-4772-6339-6 (e)*

*Library of Congress Control Number: 2012915824*

*Any people depicted in stock imagery provided by Thinkstock are models, and such images are being used for illustrative purposes only.*
*Certain stock imagery © Thinkstock.*

*This book is printed on acid-free paper.*

*Because of the dynamic nature of the Internet, any web addresses or links contained in this book may have changed since publication and may no longer be valid. The views expressed in this work are solely those of the author and do not necessarily reflect the views of the publisher, and the publisher hereby disclaims any responsibility for them.*

# CONTENTS

# DEDICATION

I want to dedicate this book to my maternal grandmother
Macie Marion Harrison Barber
Grandma, I love you with all my heart!
Your Spirit is forever present . . .

# PREFACE

I WROTE THIS book originally to give my account of dealing with Multiple Myeloma, cancer of the plasma cells. I wanted to be able to share my experiences and encourage others who may be encountering the same situation. To let you know that if I can make it with the help of the Lord, you can too. However, things happened in my life during the course of dealing with my cancer and I was swayed to also incorporate my feelings with regard to my sick grandmother, who was very close to my heart. She passed away during the writing of this book (October 2009). This played a huge role in my treatment process of the Multiple Myeloma.

My husband was also diagnosed with diabetes and was placed out of work due to being placed on insulin. I had to deal with the death of a cousin (DC) and an uncle (NY) who both passed away on Thanksgiving Day 2009. I also had another cousin to pass away just a few days before New Years.

There was a lot I had to deal with and during this time, I truly learned to depend and trust solely in God. Subconsciously, I think my mind was saying 'Okay, I'm not working, but Charles is working. So we will get by.' In my mind, I was depending on my husband to provide. Well, when he was diagnosed with diabetes and out of work, it was a rude awakening. God said 'Okay, where is your bread and butter coming from now? It's coming from the same person who will heal you of this cancer.'

I have grown up in the church. I am saved. I know that God is a healer. I know that God is a provider but because of going through this, I know that I know that I know and no one can sway me. During this time, we did not get put out of our house. We were never sent a foreclosure notice. We did not go lacking for food. We kept all of our vehicles and everything we had. Bills still got paid on time, and we got some big bills. Tell me God ain't good! I gained a greater appreciation for the saying, "That which does not kill you definitely makes you stronger". I learned that no matter how things look or how you feel, that God is ultimately in control. I realized that if you are still here, he has a plan for you.

Three years later, I can say in the words of Marvin Sapp, "I never would have made it, never could have made it, without you [God]. I'm stronger, I'm wiser, I'm better, much better." It is amazing how cancer, something that seems so near to death (and it truly is) can have such a wonderful and glorious outcome. Going through this process has truly made much better financially [believe it or not—considering all that we had to spend out and are still spending out], spiritually [my faith is so much stronger now than ever before] and physically. Hopefully, as you read my story, you will become encouraged.

"For I know the plans I have for you", declares the Lord,
"plans to prosper you and not to harm you,
plans to give you hope and a future."
Jeremiah 29:11

# ACKNOWLEDGEMENTS

- My husband and my boys—Thank you for taking care of the Deeva and Queen of the house, who has for so long, taken care of the Kings of the house and others and often times neglected herself. I love you! I love you! I love you! Thank you for sharing me with the world! I do so much for so many people and it may seem like I have you on the back burner, but I am sure that you know that I do not. Everyone knows that my family always comes first! **Pookie, thank you for loving me in sickness and in health!**

- Mommie and Daddy—I do not know what to say except I love you both more than words can ever say. You hung in there and supported me (as you both have my whole life) while both of you were taking care of your own parents.

- Cousin Edie—I know that we are cousins by blood, but I have always thought of you as my big sister. You have been there for me for everything since kindergarten graduation. I love you and I am really sorry for not telling you about the cancer in the beginning.

- All of my family (either by blood or marriage)—Thank all of you for everything! I love you all!

- Reverend Dr. Wayne Baxter, my Pastor at Oak Grove Missionary Baptist Church—you did not miss a beat—you faithfully called me twice a week, sometimes more. I still to this date, have the cactus [you know the one I finally got—(inside joke) ☺] you sent me during transplant. Thanks for always encouraging me. I love you!

- Oak Grove Church Family—Thanks for your prayers and support! I will not name anyone individually because I am sure that I will forget someone, so I say "Thank you to everyone"—You are my second family!
- Aunt Ree for going with me every Thursday to Duke for chemo. You could have been doing other things but you stayed with me.
- Nurse practitioners, doctors, custodians at Duke University Adult Bone Marrow Transplant, Gibson Cancer Center and Medical Specialists Clinic
- RCCC and RCC—Thanks for being my prayer partners from the very beginning. Thanks for getting on me when I did not post journal updates. (I know, you were only concerned about what was going on.) You attended my benefit singing. You came to see me while I was at Duke. You are all true friends!
- Bunny—Thanks for shaving my hair when finally lost it all. My hair was falling out but you helped me to keep myself all together!
- Ms. Beth Lindsey, Benefits Specialist with the Public Schools of Robeson County—Thanks for helping me with my disability papers each and every month.
- A special thanks to you and you and even you for your love, prayers, gifts, visits and support throughout this journey

# INTRODUCTION

M Y NAME IS Demetria Michele Alexander-Grissett. I am writing this book to give my personal journalized account of dealing with Multiple Myeloma, a cancer of the plasma cells. However, during the course of writing this book, other situations occurred which will leave a lasting effect on the rest of my life as well. First, I want to provide a little history about myself which may help you to understand my character much better. I am an only child born and raised in Baltimore, Maryland. My parents were divorced when I was in middle school. However, they have always maintained a friendly relationship. The majority of my family, including my father, maternal grandmother and paternal grandfather, aunts, uncles, cousins, godmother, and godsisters reside in Baltimore. My mother resides in her home of South Carolina. Some people label only children as "spoiled children".

I do not necessarily call myself spoiled. Spoiled to me is getting everything you want. Well, I guess I may have been spoiled at times. I had and continue even now to have a good life. I never gave my parents any major problems. I believe that you reap what you sow. I was not one who went out drinking, smoking and partying. I did not sleep round and have a lot of babies. I was no angel for sure, but I was your average, good, scholarly child.

Even though my parents got divorced when I was young, I still maintained communication with my father. I lived with my mother, grandmother, and favorite cousin who is like my big sister (Edie). I must tell you that I really, really, really love my grandmother and grew up being much attached to her and still to this day. Anyone who knew her knew why. I am her only grandbaby.

When I was a teenager, I could not stand for Grandma to call me "baby". One day, I told her how I disliked it and I did not want her to call me that anymore. Do you know what she told me? She said that I could be fifty years old with ten children and I would still be her baby. I thought about it. I did not quite understand it. I left it alone. She was not one with whom you could win an argument anyway. It really wasn't until I had children of my own that I truly understood what she was saying and I feel the exact same way about my own boys.

My parents gave me all of the love and inspiration that any child could ask for. The support was there for whatever I wanted to do. I was encouraged to do any and everything. I stayed very active in school and church. My parents provided guidance and love that was unmatched anywhere and I love them for that.

I was raised in the church so I guess that was why I did not have time for the drinking and smoking and other stuff. It seemed like we were in church every time the doors opened. I was on the choir. I was the church secretary. I was a Sunday School teacher, Vacation Bible School teacher, Junior missionary and usher.

My church was Christian Life Fellowship Baptist Church which evolved in the late seventies under the leadership of Elder Stanley M. Butler. We were what I call a growing church because our church was full of young people. Young people ultimately grow up to become the church of tomorrow. Many activities were provided to keep us busy. There was a Sunday out of each month designated as Youth Sunday. We all took a part in leading the church service. The youth did the devotions. A young person would do the scripture. Someone would do the prayer. The youth would sing. Someone would do the church announcements. The youth were already ushering so they took up the offering. It provided not only a spiritual foundation, but a foundation of genuine friendships that, as young people, have stuck with us to this day.

I attended the Public Schools of Baltimore City and Baltimore County. My parents expected nothing but the best and that was what I produced. I graduated from an Advanced College Preparatory Curriculum from an engineering high school. Upon graduating from high school, I made a big move and attended college in North Carolina. It was very difficult to move somewhere I had never been. It was even harder to leave my family and church friends whom I had grown up with all my life. My mother had always talked about Johnson C. Smith University (JCSU) so I did the application just to keep her quiet.

It was at Johnson C. Smith University (Charlotte, North Carolina) that I did my undergraduate study and later my graduate study at Fayetteville State University (Fayetteville, North Carolina). I received my Bachelor of Science degree in Computer Information Systems/Business (Cum Laude) and my Masters Degree in Business Administration with a concentration in Management. I had always wanted to go back home after my undergraduate studies but it just never seemed to work out to be able to secure a job. Baltimore is such a metropolitan area. However, attending Johnson C. Smith and staying in Charlotte was one of the best decisions I had ever made.

Just as my cousin/sister (Edie) at home, I pledged Zeta Phi Beta Sorority, Inc. in the Fall 1989 semester. Yes, I said pledged. We did some things that I do not know if it is legal to write on these pages. Our line name was "The Fugitives". That was because we always did our best to run away to get out of doing things. I was #3—Rock Master. I developed a very special bond with my three line sisters (#1—Quiet Storm, #2—NWA {Nigger with an attitude}). They are my true sisters. They always got my back. To this date, some twenty years later, that bond continues to grow stronger.

At JCSU, I did work study in the Student Financial Aid Office. Because I applied to the school late, I was awarded my financial aid very late in the semester. All of the work study positions were filled. I was sent to this place, that place and this place. Only to be turned away from all of them.

The work study coordinator had a discussion with the Financial Aid Director. I could imagine her saying "Look, this poor child has been everywhere on campus. There are no more open positions. Do you think she can work here?" They took a big chance with me and said that I could work in the Financial Aid Office. They would try me out. Oh, they were hesitant, I'm sure. They already had an office full of students working in the Financial Aid Office. I could not fault them. You are working with sensitive financial information. You get information in the wrong hands and the wrong students can spread information about other students. Trouble! Trouble! They tried me out and have yet to regret it.

Little did I know then that this would turn into a career for me. I truly had a passion for what I did and people came to me because I showed genuine compassion. I helped everyone. Someone helped me and I was always brought up to help people when you can. You never know when you are going to need someone else's help. You have to crawl before you can walk. I began as a work-study student and was hired full-time, the semester before graduation, four years later. I worked in financial aid at JCSU for ten years (serving in several positions to include a work study student, secretary and federal work study coordinator).

I only stayed on campus (Sanders Hall Room 418) the first semester of my freshman year. I just could not cope with not having a front door key to the dorm building. I had to share four payphones with a floor of forty girls. That's right. We had no front door keys to the building nor did we have individual phones in the rooms. (Oh no!) And the eating hours were out of my range—dinner is over at six, what? I am hungry again around eight or nine. So, I had to move. I had moved into two different apartments before one of my sisters and I moved into an apartment. It was there that I met a gentleman whom I always tried to avoid. We were neighbors at the apartment complex. He and I were both involved with others at the time. Seems like we always ran into each other in the parking lot or at the mailbox at the same time all of the time. I can remember times I would leave work late just so I could not run into him at home. Somehow it still seemed like I would run into him. I do not know what it was, but I knew I did not like him.

Two years later, I married that man, Charles Grissett. He was from Lumberton, North Carolina, a very rural area. He is from the country, point blank. Sometimes we do not see eye to eye with things and that is just because we are from two very different areas. I can recall when we were looking for a house in Charlotte; what was space to me was too close to him. I grew up in the city in a rowhouse and he grew up having a lot of land surrounding him. That was a challenge for us!

We have two handsome sons. Our first son has his name (Charles Grissett, Jr.—known as CJ) and the second son (Demetrius Michael) has his birth date, but was named after me. (I had to get something out of it, don't you think?) My name is Demetria Michele and his name is Demetrius Michael.

At the time we got married, I worked in financial aid at Livingstone College as the Financial Aid Computer Coordinator. Two years following, I began working as the Financial Aid Specialist at Central Piedmont Community College. In 2000, shortly after the birth of our second son, we left Charlotte, NC and moved to Lumberton, NC. Charles thought Charlotte was too fast. I thought Charlotte was too slow. He thought that raising the boys up in a rural environment would be much better than in the city, although crime is everywhere now.

I was blessed to continue working in the area of financial aid when we moved to Lumberton. Charles had no problem adjusting because he was a self-employed truck driver. I applied for a financial aid position at the University of North Carolina at Pembroke (UNCP). I was truly over-qualified for the position. But I was offered and accepted the position. The position was half the pay I was receiving in Charlotte. But hey, I said you have to crawl before you walk. Sometimes you have to get your foot in the door to be able to get where you want to go. I know in my heart that they were pleased with the level of professionalism that I gave. This I could tell because of how the Director really tried to keep me when I made a decision to leave. They could not match the position monetarily, though they negotiated rigorously. Distance also played a huge factor. I felt that I needed to be closer to home.

I left UNCP and was employed in financial aid at Robeson Community College in Lumberton, NC. I worked there for four years until 2005 at which time I began working for the Public Schools of Robeson County. I had just received my Masters Degree from Fayetteville State University in May 2005. As a child, I always said that I wanted to be a teacher. I guess when you look at it; I still remained in the area of education. I just went from college level students to a younger group of students.

I had worked in financial aid for eighteen years and it was time for a change. I began working as a Special Populations Coordinator at Fairmont High School. In this position, I ensured that members of special populations (economically and academically disadvantaged students) gained equal access to, progressed through and succeeded in the Career and Technical Education (CTE) programs. CTE programs include Career Development, Allied Heath Sciences, Family and

Consumer Sciences, Agricultural Education, Marketing Education, Business and Information Technology, and Trade and Industrial courses.

Due to certification issues, I was transferred to the local vocational and technical high school, Robeson County Career Center, as a Network Engineering teacher. The following year, I worked as a Career Development Coordinator. In this position, I provided a variety of career guidance services including helping students develop and implement an individual career development plan with the ultimate goal being to help students make good decisions about themselves and their future. I was employed in this position from 2006 until the beginning of the 2009-2010 academic year. A lot of things happened at the beginning of the 2009-2010 academic year. And this is where my real story begins.

I have always had excellent health up until . . .

# MY STORY

IN MAY 2008, during a routine doctor's visit, my blood work showed that my white blood cell count was low. The doctor said it was nothing to be alarmed about at the time, but would continually be looked at during future visits. For a year, my counts had increased at one point, then decreased, increased again, and then decreased continually. After several tests, my primary care physician referred me to specialists at a Blood Disorder Clinic at the local Cancer Center (Gibson Cancer Center).

I can remember the nurses saying how positive my attitude was. They would say "When some people come here, they come in crying. They do not know how to react after being told that they have cancer." I replied "Why should I come in crying? I don't have cancer. I have some type of blood disorder. That is why I am here." That is what I was told. My blood needed to be looked at more deeply.

I would go to the doctor at least once a week. Nothing definitive would ever come about from these visits. However, you could tell that something was wrong. After each visit, Charles would always ask "What did the doctor say today?" I would tell him that they would say something is wrong with me but they cannot say for sure because I do not really show any signs or symptoms. The word myeloma came up in conversation. This was known as the "elderly' disease. There were no cases of anyone having myeloma under age sixty. Well, I am forty. That's number one. My age is saying I should not have it. They also state that I should be in a lot of pain. I am in no pain. Things were like normal if you were to ask or look at me.

You hear doctors mumbling and you pray that you do not have cancer. It is hard to not think about it when things look so bleak and discouraging. It would seem like it is something serious because why else would you go to the doctor as often as once or twice a week. Yet, they are constantly saying that I do not have any symptoms. I went back and forth to the doctor. The doctor would say that my file and bloodwork is confusing to them. After more tests, the oncologists and doctors sent my medical records to Duke University Medical Center in Durham, North Carolina for a second opinion.

They told me that I have the doctors at Gibson and Duke scratching their heads. They studied my family history very thoroughly. They have given me test after test after test. The word 'myeloma' still came up in discussion, but they said that I could not have this—I am in excellent health otherwise and this occurs in elderly people aged sixty and older. This was very difficult to understand since no one in my family has ever had any type of cancer. They would say that I should be feeling very tired all of the time. I should be in a lot of pain. If you know me, you know that I am never tired. How can I be? I am football mom, soccer mom, baseball mom, and basketball mom, just to start the list off.

I had to have a bone marrow biopsy. Oh that is the worse. Let me explain this process to you. The area is numbed to the bone by placing a long needle into the hip area. The white blood cells are manufactured in the bone marrow. Therefore, they go into the bone and get this fluid (marrow) from the bone. Nope, they are not finished. Then they have to go back in and cut a piece of the actual bone. Then they take "this stuff" and study it to try to come to a definitive medical conclusion. The bone marrow biopsy still could not provide any conclusive information.

Well, they had my medical records so now the doctor at the Gibson Cancer Center referred *me* (actual person and not me on paper) to Duke University Medical Center. Well, I did not mind because they are like the research capitol of what . . . the world? They did inform me that I would probably have to have a more intensive bone marrow biopsy, along with a bone survey, . . . basically, all of the work I already had done, but they stated that the tests at Duke would be more intense. Is 'intense' another word for 'hurt more'?

I looked up this 'myeloma' on the internet. I am always one who researches things. I do not take someone's word for anything. I like to find out for myself. The thing I read was that myeloma is treatable, but not curable.

I was sent to Clinic 1B/1C at the Duke University Medical Center. Charles went with me on this initial visit. It was June 17, 2009. Upon my arrival, they take fifteen vials of blood from me. Yes, fifteen! I asked the lady if she would leave me some blood. Couldn't she see how small I was? She stated that usually for an initial patient examination, twenty-three vials of blood are taken. I told her to proceed and was appreciative that I was only giving fifteen. Everyone in the office laughed.

From there, I proceeded upstairs to Radiology where I was given a bone survey. Oh, let me explain that I was told that I was going to have to give blood. Well, you know how with some blood work that you must fast the night before. I was not told prior to my visit if I should have fasted before hand. I did not eat after midnight just to be safe.

Okay, so back to the bone survey. This is an x-ray of every bone in my entire body. They took close to twenty plus slides. This is to determine whether cancer has spread from the original site to the bones. They also look for holes in my bones, or osteolytic lesions, which are caused by myeloma cells in the bone marrow.

After a couple of slides, the room began to get hot to me. I got very sweaty and passed out. The nurse said that my sugar was either too high or too low, or it may have been my blood pressure. I don't really remember. I was out. I explained to them that I had not eaten. They told me that I could have and should have eaten. Now they tell me.

They immediately gave me some crackers and orange juice. Once my vital signs returned to normal, I was given the rest of my bone survey lying down. We proceed back downstairs to the initial area where we would meet with the doctor. Neither Charles nor I knew what to expect. What was told to us though would change the rest of our lives.

We were brought into a room. We were in there alone for a while. I called the veterinarian to check on "Snoop", my Yorkshire terrier. He was really sick. I had my mind on "Snoop" to divert my own personal feelings with all of this medical stuff. The doctor finally came in and he began to discuss the results of my bloodwork and explained what myeloma was. Just about all of what he explained was not foreign to me, as I had read most of it during my research. The doctor explained everything in depth. He would explain it and look at us very intensely and pause for five seconds. I don't know if he was making sure that we were digesting the information or was he waiting for us to show some emotion or waiting for a response. I don't know. It was truly a lot to digest. He gave me a pathology report and officially diagnosed me with 'Multiple Myeloma', a cancer of the plasma cells.

In Multiple Myeloma, normal plasma cells, an important part of the immune system, transform into malignant myeloma cells. These malignant cells multiply and grow at a rapid rate crowding out the production of normal blood cells and antibodies in the bone marrow. These malignant cells have no purpose whereas the white blood cells, which are decreasing, are very important to our body to fight off infections.

To hear the words 'You have cancer' and to hear of so many people dying of cancer, I simply cannot put into words the empty feeling that I felt. When you are given a pathology report, it is like being given a death certificate only you are still alive. It is as if they are saying "you are about to die, but we do not know exactly when. So we want your life to be as comfortable as possible."

I was told that my life expectancy was five years. He explained to us that Multiple Myeloma is treatable, not curable and that their goal is to provide treatment that would give me an enjoyable and comfortable quality of life for the remaining time I have left. I was given options which were inclusive of various drugs to take (including chemotherapy and/or radiation treatments). Another option was a bone marrow stem cell transplant. The doctor proceeded to tell us about all of the options in depth.

Regarding the bone marrow stem cell transplant, the doctor suggested that we make an appointment with the Adult Bone Marrow Transplant (ABMT) Department to get more information. He referred us to a doctor who was the best and was known nationally and internationally for Multiple Myeloma research. Charles said if that doctor was the best, then that is who he wanted me to see. From having information on all options, we can make a more decisive choice as to what route I need to take.

I was told that I would have to have another bone marrow biopsy. Okay, Gibson Center did tell me this. I told the doctor that I was ready for that, not knowing that he was talking about having it immediately, like right then and there. Charles said it made sense to do it now since we were already there. We would not have to make another two hour drive (one way) just for that. Easy for him to say, he was not the one getting stuck in the butt.

I told the doctor that I only had one request. I was hungry. I wanted to eat. Mind you, I still had not eaten since midnight the night before, except for the crackers and juice they gave me in Radiology. It was about noon at this time. He stated that by the time we went to eat in the cafeteria, he would have time to get the tech to schedule the biopsy. We left and ate in the cafeteria. Everything was solemn. I believe Charles nor myself knew what to say to the other.

All I could think about is that what I did not want to be—**IS**. I did not want to hear that I had cancer. I did not want to believe that I had cancer. Even though I prayed and prayed and had others praying for me that I would not have cancer, the fact remained and was confirmed that I had cancer. When do you stop praying that you do not have cancer? Even though you yourself claim that you do not have cancer, do you really believe the doctor's word or believe God?

Oh boy, is my faith being tested big time again. All I could think about is when I had two miscarriages back to back. I did not want to believe that I had a miscarriage, especially when with one pregnancy, I had ultrasound pictures. And then you tell me all of a sudden, that there is no baby. No! I refused to believe that! All of the prayer and faith did not change a thing then. Just like it did not change a thing now. I just had to face it. I had cancer! I can truly say that no one ever would want to hear those words.

I need to do a list of everything that needs to be done. Truth be told, I run the household. It reminded me of the last words I remember my best friend's mother, Moma Dot, telling me before she passed away last year, . . . that I am the glue that keeps my family together. I handle any and all paperwork with the household. I do everything but the cooking. I clean and wash and review homework and go to athletic games and the list goes on and on.

What will happen next? So many questions come to my mind. I need to crack down on my estate planning and gather insurance information together. My brain was just ticking away until I thought information was going to ooze out of my ear. What else do I need to do? Well, it was time to head back upstairs. I went back and Charles went to sit in the jeep to get some rest because he knew that he would be driving back home and I am sure he needed time for himself after getting this news.

Well, it took about two hours before I had the biopsy done. Oh, yes, this was more "intense". It hurt far more badly than the one I had done in Lumberton. The biopsy done in Lumberton was done as I was on my right side. This one was done with me lying flat on my stomach. Duke claims they get better results that way. The tech said that I had hard bones. They numbed me with no problem. Thank God! She had the hardest time trying to get to my bones though. She said I had bones the strength of a NFL player. She said that you cannot tell looking at me from the outside that my bones were as strong as they were. Me? Strong bones? Come on. I thought she would never get the needle in. Oh, she pushed and pushed and pushed. They claimed they gave me enough numbing medicine. How come I felt everything? Man, was my butt hurting. I would not wish this pain on my worst enemy.

When I had the bone marrow biopsy done at the Gibson Cancer Center, I was out of work only one day, no problem. I feel like this one will be different. The tech asked the other technician if she wanted to try. It took her forever it seemed. After about fifteen minutes, they finally got in to get what they needed. The whole process took so long that Charles began to wonder what was going on. He had been texting me. Well, my phone was in my pocket book. I could not get to it. Then I was in recovery. He had walked back to the hospital from the parking lot to check on me. Thank the Lord, by that time, I was just checking out and getting my next appointment with the Adult Bone Marrow Transplant Department. Boy, was that painful! I was out of work for three days this time. Glad school just got out.

That two hour ride home was the longest ride I can remember. It felt like six hours. I felt so bad because I was in so much pain. I was unable to attend Michael's championship baseball game tonight. Charles and the boys came home after the game. Michael, who would have otherwise been jovial, just sat down in the living room where I was with his head down. This was not his character at all.

I asked him how the game was. He replied 'Fine' with his head still down. I asked him how he did. He replied 'Alright' still with his head down. I assumed they must have lost. He stated that they won. You must understand that my youngest son, Michael, is the very out-going one; the very talkative one. He knows no strangers, like his daddy. My oldest son, CJ, had walked in the house and went straight to his room. Something was really wrong with this picture. Charles walks in the living room and Michael gets up to go and take his bath. Charles proceeds to tell me that he told the boys the news about my cancer. I had to pick my mouth up from the floor. You did what?

He said that as they came home, he told the boys that Mommie is really sick and they all need to help Mommie around the house more. I am sure that CJ understood. He's no dumb child. He's first in his class. I know that he put two and two together. Mommie had never been sick. A minor cold or a migraine headache here or there. Mommie is all of a sudden going to the doctor once or twice a week on a regular basis. I believed that Michael was too young to understand. I asked Charles if he thought that the boys understood. He thought that they did. Charles said he could tell that Michael understood just from his reactions. I guess I could too because his reactions were so unnatural. Charles said he thought it would be better if they heard it from us before they hear something in the street and the information gets misconstrued. Still . . . I could not accept all of this as an adult. How can they really understand what's going on. The doctors don't even know. This is too much for a child to take in.

Charles called CJ into the living room where we were. He wanted to know if there was anything that CJ wanted to ask me. I can remember the look CJ had on his face. It was as if it was too much for him to digest. This was very well understood. I did not want to press the issue. That was my child. This was too much for me to take. I am sure that he had questions—"Is my mommie gonna live?", "How long?" Shoot, I had those same questions and some. It was natural to have those questions. That is *"Moma's boy"* and he always will be. The house had that same solemn feeling as it did when Charles and I were coming home that evening. Little talking. There was a thick air in the house. I laid at night and wondered what was going to happen next.

School had just got out for the summer for the students. That was a good thing. I believe the Lord placed me at the Career Center because I was around some powerful praying people. We had prayer all of the time. I felt really bad because all of my co-workers and fellow teachers had prayed and prayed that I would be cancer-free and then the outcome turned out to be what they prayed that it would not be. I learned that just because the final outcome is not what you pray for does not mean that God does not hear your prayer. It seems like it was one of those situations that makes you want to question God and ask "Why?" I had to go back to work and tell my co-workers that this was not the case. I did not want them to feel like their prayers were in vain.

God has a different plan in mind for me. Throughout all of the back and forth, I had prayed for God's will to be done. Boy this was a lot to swallow though. I can remember that night how Charles just held me and cried. I let him. I didn't cry. I told him that I was strong and I was going to be alright. At least that is what I was thinking at the time. Wasn't sure if I honestly believed it myself. At this point, I was not sure how to feel.

Even though students were already out for the summer, I worked until the end of June. I was out of work the rest of that week due to the bone marrow biopsy. On June 23, 2009, I was back at Duke. We did more blood work and they set up an appointment with the Adult Bone Marrow Treatment Department to see what other options were available.

On June 24, 2009, I had oral surgery. This was something that had already been planned long before this Myeloma came about. I went to Fayetteville to have my two back wisdom teeth taken out. Why? I don't know. I got tired of them asking at every six month cleaning visit for the past nine years if I am in pain. They claimed that eventually infection would form and it would be better to get the teeth taken out. I am of the notion that if it ain't broke, don't fix it. It was suggested that before I begin chemo, I need to have this oral surgery done and have a follow up examination and make sure everything was okay prior to beginning chemo. So that had me out for the rest of the month.

The oral surgeon said that I healed up very well and more quickly than he expected. (Ain't God good?) I stayed numb in a very small area on my left side, but all is well. He said it would probably be thirty days or more before I get feeling back.

On July 1, 2009, I had my appointment with the Adult Bone Marrow Treatment Clinic. I had a chest x-ray, EKG, ANOTHER bone marrow biopsy and I gave fifteen vials of blood. Did I say that I had my THIRD bone marrow biopsy? (Not again!) It was a long day to say the least. To date, I have had three bone marrow biopsies and more blood taken from me than I feel I have to give (You know how small I am—Smile!), EKGs, Chest X-Rays, Skeletal X-Rays, Bone Surveys and the list goes on. Somehow, I know now that the word intense **does** mean it will hurt more.

After all of these tests, we go into the exam room to meet with the nurse practitioner and the doctor. It's a lot of paperwork to review and sign. She records the entire conversation on a cassette and gives to me at the end of our conversation. They say that I might get home later and have more questions as I sit and think things over. What are the chances of that happening? We then meet with the financial counselor followed by the social worker. We were given a tour of the treatment center. It felt very awkward to see all of the people with cancer, getting chemo or radiation.

I did not want to stare at them, but conversely I was. I said to myself that "I don't look like these people." All of them did not look sick. Look in the mirror. You do not look sick either, . . . but you are. Some had on masks. Some didn't. Some were in closed rooms. Some were in the open cubicles. Some were sitting up in a recliner. Some were lying down in the bed. Everyone was hooked up to something. The area is very somber.

I choose the route of participating in a clinical research study. What did this mean? Well, I would basically be a part of a research study that would help scientists and doctors to possibly find a cure for myeloma. They will study all of these different things about me and my tests and my blood and the whole nine yards. What did I have to lose? It would be great to be able to help find a cure for a disease. No, I would not get any money or name recognition from it. But who wants that? I would just be happy knowing that I was able to help. Many times in life, people want to always do something for something. It should not be like that. Sometimes people are in a situation where they need help and cannot afford to pay for it or get it. Sometimes you just have to give favors. You will never know when the tables will get turned and you will need a favor one day.

In my life, I have been known for giving a lot of favors. I'll do something for someone and they'll say 'How much do I owe you?". I'll reply "Nothing" or if the boys happen to be selling something for school, I will ask them to buy something from them. Some people say I am crazy for not charging but you know I see it like this—I get rewarded in blessings people do not even see.

So, I am about to begin chemotherapy. I always heard of this thing called chemo but did not know exactly what it is. Merriam-Webster Online Dictionary defines chemotherapy as the use of chemical agents in the treatment or control of disease (as cancer) or mental illness.[1] My chemo will involve taking two oral medicines (Dexamethasone and Cyclophosphamide) and an IV (Velcade). I will be going to Duke where they will administer these twice a week, Mondays and Thursdays.

This changes my calendar for the rest of my life. My life runs on a calendar. I have my life and my three boys' lives to juggle around. Church, appointments, civic organization meetings, rehearsals, and games to keep up with. July was already booked up with two week long job-related conferences; one in Atlanta, Georgia and one in Greensboro, North Carolina. Now, I have to cancel them. The one thing that I will have to definitely change and I don't want to is the fact that I can no longer see my dearest lady, my maternal grandmother—Grandma.

You see, for the past year, I have been going from Lumberton, North Carolina to home (Baltimore, Maryland) to see my grandmother who has been very ill. My grandmother and I are extremely close. There has not been anything that I can remember that I have ever kept from her. Until now. Ever since the very beginning of this talk about the low white blood cell count, I told my doctor that it was just stress from worrying about my grandmother. I said my count would be normal when I stop worrying about her. There may have been some physical attribution related to it, but I know that I was worried about Grandma. The time frame calculated correctly. Everything happened around the same time.

I can remember in the very beginning of my grandmother's sickness when my mother called me and I was under the hair dryer at the beauty salon. When she said that my grandmother was in the emergency room, I was ready to get up, hair dryer and all, and hit Interstate 95 Northbound. My grandmother had worked for thirty plus years at University Hospital. I have never in my life known her to be sick. Never! Sounds familiar, huh? (Like what CJ thought of me.)

She had a doctor's appointment that day and she couldn't breathe. Since then, almost a year and a half later, it has been one thing to another. She tried to keep a lot of things from the family for a very long time. I believe that she knew she was getter worse, but did not want to tell anyone. Instead of having her nieces take her to her doctor's appointment, she would ask different friends. This was so that the family could not know what the doctors said. But as you were with her at home, it was apparent that she was not acting like herself.

One thing after another happened. She had difficulty walking, difficulty breathing, difficulty hearing on one side, difficulty seeing on one side, rheumatoid arthritis kicked in, etc, etc. She already had high blood pressure and diabetes to worry about prior to this other stuff. So, for the past year, me and the boys were going home every other weekend. Visiting her every other weekend had already changed my schedule. I was no longer active in my civic and professional organizations as I had been—Johnson C. Smith University Alumni Chapter, Zeta Phi Beta Sorority, Oak Grove Missionary Baptist Church activities, etc. I just had to cut some things off.

She is the only grandmother that I have. I am the only granddaughter she has. You see, I was used to her coming to be with us for a week or so, during holidays or special times of the year or just whenever. What was I going to do now that I would not be able to see her every other weekend? I have spoiled her. She knows when to look for her boys. And she expects to see them. Sometimes she has trouble knowing what day of the week it is, but she knows when to look for her two great-grandsons—every other weekend. They are her world! (I had them for her! Those are her babies!)

Grandma gradually got to the point where she could not be alone. She needed twenty-four hour care. My two cousins had been doing what they could for so long but they have to work and have other obligations themselves. If I could do it, Heaven knows, I would.

So, in May 2009, my mom decided to pack her things in Rock Hill, South Carolina and "temporarily" move home to Baltimore. She is retired so she can do that. I am so happy because now Grandma cannot hide anything because Mommie is there. Mommie will be able to take her to her doctor's appointments and find out what the doctors are saying. She is able to make sure Grandma takes her medicines like she should. Once my cancer came about, I know that Mommie really wanted to be with me. Mommie knows that I will not be in my right mind for worrying about Grandma.

Charles had suggested that I go home that particular week because since I was going to begin chemo on July 20, 2009, I would not be able to make my usual trips home. What was I going to tell Grandma? I cannot lie to her. Well, I could tell her that since I was being transferred to a new school that I could not go home like I used to. Nah, she is too smart for that.

I would not be lying. I did get a letter about a week or so ago stating that I was being transferred to another school in the county in a different position. No longer a Career Development Counselor but back as a teacher. Due to the economy, there had been many cutbacks within the state system. There were other Career Development Counselors who were merged back into the classrooms. I was not excited about this move but hey, I was thankful just to have a job. Right now, I had more important things on my mind. I would figure out what to tell Grandma, when and if, that time came. I could, under no circumstances, tell her I had cancer. Her heart would be too weak to take the news.

Well, I did decide to make that trip home. The boys (for the first time) did not go with me. They had spent the week with my father-in-law in Florida. My father-in-law thought I might want some time to myself. I did need that. They spent the week before that in Columbia, SC with my sister-in-law. That was an unexpected and unplanned visit, but well needed for sure. My sister-in-law was pregnant at the time with my niece. She was due any day.

I cried that entire Sunday night when the boys left for Columbia. That was my time. Not because they left and I missed them. I just had my quiet moment to sit and analyze things. I can remember feeling like I cannot take this. All of this was just too much for me. I didn't know how I was going to make it. There was too much going on at one time. Grandma being sick and then this myeloma stuff. Charles held me this time and re-assured me that I was going to make it. That I am a strong woman. Everything was going to be alright. He was going to be there until the end. He reminded me that I was not in this alone. I was honest and told him that if he thought this was going to be too much for him, that he could bail out now. I was not sure if I could take it if he decided to bail out later. I assured him that I would not be mad at him. He told me that when he said those wedding vows, that he meant it and he was not going anywhere.

I heard him but I didn't hear him. My feelings were all that I felt. I felt that this was happening to no one but me. No one knows how I feel. Unless you had cancer, you could not talk to me. And I honestly did not want to talk to anyone else. I went into a seclusion stage. I did not want people to see me nor did I want to see them and have to repeat my situation and my story over and over. And there are times when you know people want to say something to you or ask questions but do not. The *air* around you just seems awkward and thick.

I went home (Baltimore) and I wondered if that was the right thing to do. It was so hard to be there and not tell Grandma or anyone else for that matter. This trip truly had an emotional toll on me. One that I was not sure that I was ready to handle. I stayed at the hospital from sun up to sun down. I would have spent the night but Grandma always would make me go home when it got dark and she made me promise to call her and let her know I made it home alright. One intention I did have for this trip was to tell my father. I hinted around about going out to eat. Nothing unusual for us. We could not work out the schedule on one particular day. We went out the next day. He picked me up from the hospital where I was with Grandma.

Grandma was in a rehab center but happen to be in the hospital at that particular time I was home. She was going back and forth often from the rehab center to the hospital and back again.

Daddy and I went to Windsor Inn to eat. I tried to, near the end of our meal, ask about my grandfather's health. You see, my paternal grandfather is also ill. I asked my father what was my grandfather's medical history. I asked this for two reasons: one because I wanted to confirm what I told the doctors that no cancer ran in my family and second, this was going to be a bridge into the conversation of telling him about the cancer.

As I asked him, he replied, "Well, he began at MeHarry Medical ..." and I interrupted and told him I did not want to know *that* medical history. My grandfather was a dentist so my dad was about to give me his educational medical history. I told him I wanted to know his medical history as far as sickness. He and my maternal grandmother both had high blood pressure and diabetes. All of this I knew. This was kind of a double confirmation that cancer did not run on my daddy's side of the family.

At that point, I could not tell him still. But I knew I had to tell him while sitting down. We had been in the restaurant for a while just talking and watching the wide screen. We left and I wondered how I was going to tell him. As he was driving me back to the hospital, I told him that when we arrive at the hospital, that I had to tell him something so I did not want him to just drop me off and yet I did not want him to go in the hospital with me because I couldn't tell him while in Grandma's room.

Of course, our conversation got quiet. I could feel him trying to think about what I was going to tell him. I told him, "Stop trying to think. I'll tell you when we get there." He just smiled and said okay yet still trying to figure out in his mind what I was going to tell him. He pulled up at the front entrance of the hospital and parked. Why did he do that? Why didn't he just park in a parking space? Now, I have to tell him in front of these people as they are walking in and out of the hospital.

I began to tell him the reason why I asked him what I asked him as far as my grandfather. Then I bridged the conversation to tell him why I asked. Well, needless to say, my father did not take it well at all. I am so glad that I did not tell him while we were driving. We would have surely had an accident. What can you expect; as I said before, I am the only child, the baby. Deep down inside, I felt like he probably thought that I was going to tell him that I was pregnant or something. He was probably looking for some type of positive news. I know that he never would have expected the news I gave him.

I did everything to hold back tears and he did too. I told him everything from the beginning to the present. I told him about how I was home now because I was about to start my chemotherapy treatments and who knows when I would be able to come back home. That was the hardest thing I have ever had to tell my dad. Boy, I wish I would have never had to tell him any news like that. He said he did have some errands to run but now he could not go anywhere. He said he just had to go home. I could understand. I told him to call me as soon as he got home. I was so worried about him driving home with this news on his mind. I wondered if I had made the right direction to tell him like I did. I made him promise that he would call me when he got home. And he did.

I had to get myself together as I went into the hospital. I stayed with Grandma in the hospital everyday while I was home. I did not want to leave her side. It hurts so bad to know that I cannot tell her. For those who know our relationship, you can understand why this is hard for me to deal with. I have always told Grandma everything. I cannot think of anything that I have not ever told her. And if I did not tell her something, she could tell when something is wrong, just by my voice, just by talking to me or looking at me. Many times my mother found out things about me from my Grandma. Everybody knows the relationship we have. Everyone!!!

You know it is a lot dealing with the cancer and then to deal with a sick grandparent. Words cannot express. All I can say is, if you haven't gone through it, you just don't know nor can you imagine. You just cannot talk to me. Plain and simple. I could not tell anyone else, not even my close cousin, Edie. Until this stuff got digested within myself, I just could not tell anyone.

Well, my trip was over. I left Baltimore and was lead to hit I-85 Southbound toward Charlotte. It was on my heart to tell my two sisters, Artie and Venita. Yes, I told you I was an only child. My two sorority sisters are my two best friends (true sistas) since college. One is originally from New York and the other from Pittsburgh. There is another one from New York whom we lost touch with a few years after graduation. We all graduated together and managed to become productive citizens of Mecklenburg County, until, of course, I broke the chain and moved to Robeson County (Lumberton). I do not know to this day if those girls ever forgave Charles for doing that? (Things that make you go 'Hum?')

Distance does not separate us though. That's what we have cell phones for, right? Yes, I have always been known to get in a car and go. Driving is nothing to me. I cannot not help but travel. I was on the hip of Grandma everywhere and that woman traveled. So, after that eight hour drive, I arrived in Charlotte. I wanted to tell them both together. Well, Artie had just had a wisdom tooth taken out. She was doped up when I called her so I decided to let her sleep. After having my two wisdom teeth out less than a month ago, I know the pain she was feeling. I got Venita and we went to Quinzo's to eat. I did not know Quinzo's was that good. It was my first time eating there. It was delicious. We ate inside. Afterwards, we sat in the car and tried to contact Artie but could not get her and we assumed that she was sleep.

My girls know that when I call a meeting, it is serious. So, Venita was getting on my nerves trying to figure out what the news was that I had to tell them. Just a month ago, her family and my family and some others went on a cruise to the Bahamas during Memorial Weekend. I knew the news somewhat then but I told her that I did not want to mess up the trip for anyone.

This has always been the "tough" sister. I cannot remember the last time that I ever saw her cry, if I ever have in the twenty plus years that we have been together. When I told her in the car, she lost it. She's detailed oriented like myself so she wanted to see paperwork and she asked me fifty million questions. She called Artie waking her up crying and begging her if we can see her for just five minutes. She knew we were not gonna be there no five minutes. Not like we talk!

Artie is the "relaxed" sister who makes you sit back and analyze situations. She keeps us together. We would have been a wreck (all of us) if Artie had lost it also. She listened and looked at the paperwork and she had experienced a lot having recently lost her mother. She sat and listened and let me talk and Venita vent and cry. It was all good!

I needed that. Those are my ride-or-die girls. If I need them, they will come two hours to see about me. Those girls are my rock. I do not get to show it all the time. I do not call as often as I should or visit like I want. You know when you got a family and have kids that are in everything, it leaves no space or time for yourself. Those girls are my foundation and I love them both for that!

Charles also came through Charlotte to pick up his truck. He got a little ill because we did not leave Charlotte until very late. I tried to explain to him that I was fine. He was concerned because I had such a long drive by myself. It's not like it was the first time, nor will it be the last. I have learned that there are some things you must do emotionally that will help you physically. This weekend was one of them. I had to let my sistas know what was going on. Up until now, I really had not told anyone myself because I had not felt comfortable. You have to be in my comfort circle, sort of speak, for me to be able to discuss something like this with you. I just wished that I could go through this with no problem and not having to tell anyone. I wish I could keep it a secret. That would be difficult being in the small rural area in which we live.

Charles really got ill when I could not sleep any that night. My legs were just so jittery all night. I literally did not sleep. He claimed it was because I did all that driving. That driving was nothing. It was not like I had to rush home. I did not have any babies crying at home. He could not wait to go to Duke to tell on me. But come to find out, it was a symptom of the myeloma. They did not go into deep detail or specifics. I know that this was something I never had before.

While at Duke, they told me about a website service called "CaringBridge" that assists families with life-threatening situations to be able to tell their story. CaringBridge is a free personalized website service that connects family and friends during a serious health event. It makes it easier to share health updates and receive messages of love and support. First of all, I am a 'techie' up and down. This was already appealing to me because I would be at the computer anyway and not really doing anything else. Second, I loved it because it would save me from telling my story over and over and over again. You can upload photos. It has three sections—my story (where I can place my story of what happened), my journal (where I can place journal entries on a daily, weekly, or however long basis to keep people informed of my status during my treatments) and my guestbook (where visitors can sign the guestbook and leave messages). Wow, I loved it!

I began right away setting up my website. I placed my story. I decided that I would do journal entries on Mondays and Thursdays, the days I have my chemo. I may do it more or less often when something major occurs. The messages people left were inspirational. People said that I was being inspirational to them. I did not feel like that at all. They were encouraging me. It became part of my daily routine to check the guestbook and to see what people wrote.

This website is great and really helped me a lot. I am getting tired of telling people the same thing over and over again. Just record my voice and press play, will you. I realize that people are concerned (and some nosey) and want to know, but sometimes your spirit can get down as you repetitively tell your story.

There is a minimum of four to a maximum of eight cycles of chemo to be given. A cycle lasts three weeks. On days one, eight and fifteen, I have my IV chemo (Velcade) and ten pills of Dexa and sixteen pills of Cyclo. On days four and eleven, I just have my IV chemo (Velcade). Days sixteen through twenty-one are what they call my resting days. They cannot tell me at this point how many cycles I will need to complete. At the end of each cycle, I will be 're-staged' where they will look at my labwork and see where my counts are to tell if I need another cycle.

## *July 18, 2009*

Charles' grandmother passed away in March of this year. Her birthday was in July. The family decided to have an annual cookout in July in her honor. We hosted the very first one. Charles was thinking about canceling the whole thing. I guess he felt that I would not be up to it. They had been planning this since she passed away. I did not want him to cancel and then the questions would come up—why? Then I would have to tell everyone about the cancer. I did not feel like having to hear all of the fuss.

Charles thought that, because of the newly diagnosed case, that maybe we should not have all of the people over. I said let's take it in stride. Some family members knew and some did not. The only thing I was worried about is that I did not want my sister-in-law to find out. She is due any day. I did not want her to walk by someone and hear something about me. Then she would really have my niece early.

## July 20, 2009

Today was the first day of chemo. It was an interesting day! My Velcade (IV chemo) was no problem and very quick. Yee-pee. My oral chemo is another story. I have to take ten pills of Dexamethasone (Dexa) and sixteen pills of the Cyclophospamide (Cyclo). Why are the ten pills the size of a Sudafed tablet and the sixteen pills giant sized horse pills? Why couldn't it be reversed?

Do you know how long it took to take that Cyclo? Michael came with me and was a big help alternating the pill bottle and Sprite soda with me. He got tired around the tenth pill and left me to get on the laptop (If his facial expression could speak, it would probably say "Mommie, you are on your own now. I'm tired!") Plus there is the anti-nausea and anti-viral meds I have to take. So, now I am taking what a total of thirty plus pills? They say, this is an 'elderly' person's cancer. Boy, do I feel elderly now, having to keep up with all of these meds. I was so nervous trying to count out the first ten pills (They were small, I was going to take those first), that I jumped and spilled them. They had to order me six more.

They said the Dexa will give me a lot of energy—that I will probably be up tonight washing dishes and cleaning the house. Please, that's normal for me. I am feeling okay. Got a little light headed, hot and sweaty after they hooked up that IV. I don't do blood and needles well at all. The longest part is the wait. They will do bloodwork at the very beginning of each visit to see what my white blood cell count is. It must be at a certain level before they can even approve me to begin chemo. They stated that there may be times when I may come and then get turned around, if my blood count is not up far enough. Can you imagine a four hour drive for nothing? Yeah, right. My count is gonna be up there every time buddy! I have to get up too early in the morning to just turn back around.

## *July 21, 2009*

The chemo must not have kicked ALL the way in. Last night was horrible. My body ached all night. Well, not necessarily ached but felt funny and jittery all night. They said that the Dexa would have me up during the night wanting to clean the house, wash clothes, do the dishes, etc. She was right. I didn't do any of those things, but I sure couldn't sleep. I probably got two hours sleep. Not feeling as great as I did yesterday, but surely not how I felt all last night. It is evident that my body is going through some changes and it's trying to adjust like I am.

## *July 23, 2009*

Today is day four of Cycle one. I just had my Velcade (IV chemo). It was okay. I'm doing well. I'm just very tired (that's not me at all!) because along with the Myeloma (low <u>white</u> blood count), I am now anemic (due to low <u>red</u> blood cell count). This is really going to get some taking used to. No, it hasn't slowed me down any, PLEASE!!! I had to remind everyone on my CaringBridge website to send me some jokie-jokes. Everyone was getting "too spiritual". I had to remind everyone, as I previously stated, that I am saved and I know that all things work together for the good to them who love the Lord.

I know that none of this was an accident. I check the guestbook everyday. I want to read something that will make me laugh. Thank you Shelly for being the "heathen" of the group and breaking away from the spiritual words and making me laugh. Her words came right on time. I needed that! I realize that the news has knocked a lot of people off their feet and many people do not know how to respond to me. There are many people, it seems, who are avoiding me on purpose. Maybe they just do not know what to say if they see me. Trust and believe, I understand. Having this cancer is bad enough to deal with. I always try to add humor to my journal entries so I just expect to see and read the same. Yes—to my loving sista, Venita, now rest IS in my vocabulary. Only temporary, until all of this is over (Smile!)

## July 26, 2009

Today was a good day. It had nothing to do with my treatment and then it had EVERYTHING to do with it. On Friday, July 24th at 11:49 am, my sister-in-law, Angie, had a baby girl named Kylan Madison Stone. She was 5 lbs. 14 oz. and 19 ½ inches long. What? As big as my sister-in-law was? They better check and see if there is another baby up in there. Angie was too big for Kylan to just be five pounds. Well, I guess now we will tell her the news. We had decided not to tell her because she was too close to her delivery date. We did not want to jeopardize anything. This is my first (and according to her, my only) niece.

This has done me good. My emotions are really high right now. I have waited a long nine months for "Baby Girl". About an hour after she was born, I had pictures of her all over my Facebook profile. We wasted no time heading to Columbia, South Carolina for the weekend. Angie told me that I made her baby a lap happy baby in one day. Well, I am guilty as charged. That is my job as the proud auntie—to spoil the baby. She is the new delight in my life and I love her. Boy, she has given me a burst of energy that I will need for tomorrow's treatment.

## July 27, 2009

Today's treatment was good. It felt different without the boys being here. I did not have Michael to do the assembly line thing and switch back and forth giving me the Sprite bottle and the pill, the Sprite bottle and the pill. CJ had football practice at school. Charles was playing Solitaire on the laptop and I was cool with that. He needs to keep his mind occupied. He has been a great trooper through everything and I love him for that! He helped put all sixteen of those horse pills in the pill bottle. That was the worse!!! (Yuk!) Those ten pills are easy along with however many other pills.

Last night went better than last Monday night. I was not AS jittery and AS tingly and numbing as last Monday night. I do have to drink more to urinate more frequently. I appreciate everyone who sees me out and about (when I am able to go out) and tells me that I look so good. It's nothing but God!

## *July 28, 2009*

I need to catch up on things like checking my student's assignments from Friday until now. Since I was in Columbia, SC the entire weekend with my niece, I did not check any assignments. I teach an online class (Career Management) to students in all of the high schools in this county. We currently have summer school going on. This keeps my mind pre-occupied. This is very good for me now.

## *July 30, 2009*

Today's treatment was okay. Aunt Ree and Michael went with me today. CJ had driving today (Yee-pee) and Charles had to work. I told him that I'm okay. He doesn't have to go with me every Monday and Thursday. Shoot, somebody gotta work—you know what I'm saying! So, his aunt will go with me on Thursdays and he will go on Mondays. Computers were down all over Duke Hospital today so my labs had to be handwritten and then we had to wait longer than the usual hour to get the results back. Of course, this made the whole trip longer than usual.

Time flew by as Aunt Ree and I talked about life in general and people in general. Next thing we know a gentleman comes and introduces himself as Thomas and pulled up a seat and sat with us. Thomas is a 37 year old built black man who is a survivor of myeloma. He sat and just shared his experiences. He started out with plasmacyctoma (tumor in one particular area). For him, it was in his left back area. He took radiation and that went away. Sometime later he developed myeloma which is basically the same thing but it's not contained in one area—it's all over. That's why it's called *Multiple* Myeloma. He shared his experiences with chemo with the Myeloma and his transplant experiences, yes with an S. After his first transplant, he got an infection and had to have another one. Even though he came uninvited by me, I really enjoyed his company. He has an awesome personality and is full of charisma.

I know some people have different views on why certain things happen in life to certain people. Things do not always happen to you because of a punishment for something you did. Think about the story in the Bible when the man was sick and people stopped and asked him what did you or your parents do for this to happen to you. He nor his parents did anything wrong. He replied that what had happened to him was for God's glory.

I was this man last week when someone posed the question to me (out of love and concern and I appreciate them for it!). Just to assure everyone. My faith is grounded and rooted in the Word of God. (If you don't know, you better ask somebody!). Sure, I questioned God before anyone else. I put him in a corner and said "Why me?" His response to me was, "Why not you?" I'm about to do a great work and I want to use you. I think back and reflect as to when I have asked God for a certain thing. You have to remember that sometimes we may get what we want but not in the package we expect. God is using me to show his glory to someone else. He has already shown it to me and y'all I am fine. Many ask how I can take this so good and many make remarks about how good I look when they see me. It's all God!!! I feel chosen.

Have you ever done something and really did not know why you did it, and later you say "AHHHH". Believe it or not, God prepared me for this in 2006. I did something in 2006 . . . that I had no clue why, but I just listened to the voice of God and did what I was told. Two years ago, there was a teacher at my school. The day after we had the insurance representative at our school for open enrollment, he had a stroke. So, that following year, at the next open enrollment, I was led to add cancer insurance and disability insurance. I didn't know why. I just did. No one in my family has cancer so why get it? That would have been more money on my paycheck if I did not get it. I don't know. I just did as the Spirit told me to do.

I look back now and can say "Hallelujah!!!" What would happen if I did not have insurance? I cannot even imagine. You guys just wait. God is going to show himself. He already is. He is changing the minds of those who do not believe in His power. I know what God can do. He doesn't have to prove himself to me. I don't know what more I can tell you other than just enjoy the ride and watch God move. I didn't mean to get on a preaching tip. (I'm getting like Michael now) Let's open up to Psalms 100! Okay, okay!

Well, after coming home today, the chemo had me out until around seven pm. I just finished washing Snoop (my yorkshire terrier) and then I washed, dried and styled my hair. It's 9:49 pm now. I need to take my shower and grade some assignments. I haven't done that in two days. I gotta get up early in the morning again to pick up my Daddy from the Raleigh/Durham Airport. He'll be spending the weekend with us! I am so excited! Anyway, I had to get all of that out because it was for someone to read and digest all that I have said. Just as God brought Thomas to me to encourage me, I hope my words will encourage you. When God tells you to do or say something, you better do or say whatever it is.

I picked up Daddy Friday morning. We had fun this past weekend including going to CJ's church basketball game. It felt good to have all five of my favorite men with me (my husband, my father, my father-in-law and my two boys). It has been a while since my dad has been here. We all had an awesome time. Since this journey, I know that it has taken my dad for a loop—as it has alot of people. I'm 40 and I'm Daddy's Little Girl. I love my dad. He means the world to me.

He and Michael went with me to treatment. CJ had football practice and his last two (out of six) hours to get in for drivers ed (Whee-whoo!). *Permit, here we come!!!*

We got there and guess what? I did not have my IV chemo—Whew! I had my two oral chemos. I had to look back at my chart and they were right. I have my oral chemos on days one, eight, and fifteen and my IV chemo on days one and eight, I think (Oh, I forgot already—something like that) Days sixteen through twenty-one are resting days—no oral or IV chemo, which means I do not go to treatment this Thursday.

You know, for about the past year, I had been going home [Baltimore] because my dearest lady, my Grandma, has been very sick. Well, since all of this has happened. I haven't been home in maybe what six weeks. She has been hollering to see the boys before school begins. How, God worked that out! This was the perfect opportunity to go home. So after going up 95 to Duke, we had to back down 95 to Lumberton to get CJ and then me, my dad, CJ and Michael headed back up 95 South to go home.

Now, I have been driving home every other weekend for about a year now. We have been doing it for six hours easy! No problems! Why did it take us nine, almost ten, hours yesterday (on treatment day, Ohh!) We encountered several construction sites. We were stuck in one for fifty minutes and the other for almost two hours. It was crazy. We left Lumberton around three thirty pm and got home about one this morning. It's all good! We are home and I am happy. Grandma is finally home so we do not have to rush as before to go and see her at the Rehab Center. No, she still doesn't know anything and I want it to stay that way. Her heart is too weak to take it. Man, my heart can barely take all of this.

You know I like the CaringBridge website. Some people have been posting in the guestbook which I love. It allows others to see and people are not only encouraging me but someone else. Ain't that what this journey is all about? Some have been sending personal emails via my AOL account and that's fine too! Whatever tickles your fancy. Well, I have been upstairs on this computer for a minute. I know Grandma is hollering downstairs for me so I better go. Just wanted to tell everyone thanks for your encouraging words and for hanging in there with me! I'm about to starve. Gotta go!!!

My mother-in-law spent the week in Columbia to be with Angie. We had decided that it was time to tell her the news. My mother-in-law gave Angie my CaringBridge website address and told her to just look up the website. She did not look at it right away. I got a call from her and my heart dropped because I thought that she saw the website. Well, she hadn't. We were just talking about the baby. It was not until late that evening when my mother-in-law just came out and told her. Angie went to the website immediately then. My mother-in-law told me that Angie just cried because, of course, when she pulls up the website, she sees the journal entry and picture of Kylan. My mother-in-law said that as she read the journal entry, she would cry more and cry harder. I am so glad that I was not there. I am very emotional. I would not have been able to handle it. We talked later and I had to re-assure her that everything was going to be alright.

## *August 10, 2009*

Today would have been day one of cycle two. We went and as usual they took my blood and I have to wait an hour to get the results back before they can tell me if they can do the chemo. Unfortunately, I did not have my chemo today. My blood count was too low (nine hundred) to get treatment. This was what they warned me about before—that there may be times that I would get turned around. It needs to be at least a thousand before they can begin treatment. Being at nine hundred makes me more prone to infections. Right now, I cannot be around anyone who is sick, make sure everyone in the house constantly washes their hands (duh, like we don't do that already!), etc. I go back next Monday—same time, same place! I guess no news is good news, huh?

## *August 17, 2009*

Angie and Kylan came for the week. We are having a baby shower for her on next Saturday. Angie and Michael came with me to Duke today. My mother-in-law was watching our baby. Little did we know that we were going to be at Duke longer than expected. We got there at ten am (my usual time). You know I have to get the blood drawn and they have to check my blood count and all that other good stuff.

My blood count was not nine hundred like last week. It wasn't a thousand either though. It did increase to nine eighteen. [That's my house number at home in Baltimore. I need to play that number.] Everything else looked great and my doctor contacted the doctor over Millenium (sponsor for the clinical trial in which I am participating) to see if he would make an exception for me and allow me to get the chemo looking at all other factors.

That was at eleven am. I am usually getting chemo around elevenish and walking out of the door around twelvish. Around twelvish, they informed me that the doctor was in a meeting and they were sure that he would approve it, but of course you need things in black and white these days to keep yourself covered. They asked if we wanted to get something to eat and come back and go to the treatment room. Hey, this was a promotion, because all of this time we had been in the exam room with no TV (we lucked out Daddy that day we had the exam room with the TV!)

None of us were really hungry. We got some snacks thinking 'okay, maybe we won't have to wait much longer'. We were in an empty treatment room—(something different). I am so used to seeing people with whom I have connected these past three weeks. This was near the end of the day. Because there was no body heat, there was NO HEAT. We like to froze in there. My sister-in-law keeps it cold at her house and when she was cold, I knew it was COLD!!

Thank the Lord for the heated blankets they give you. Angie, Michael and I were all bundled up. Brrrhhh! Finally, around late two-ish, I was approved for my chemo. Yes, two-ish! Well, hallelujah!! So, I had to take my usual ten tiny pills, sixteen horse pills, my IV chemo, and IV potassium (yes, something new). Oh yeah, I didn't mention that my potassium was low. I'm not sure if I mentioned that two weeks ago. I have been eating bananas since then. They gave me a list of things to take that will increase my potassium. I have always been taking my blood pressure pill and potassium pill before any of this ever started. They said in taking chemo that one of your electrolytes will be bothered and it will be your magnesium or potassium. For me it is my potassium. So they have increased my potassium pills from ten mg to twenty mg.

Well, we did not leave Duke until three twenty pm. Incredible! Of all days when my sister-in-law goes with me for the first time, everything seems to be so screwed up. We stayed practically all day. We froze to death. Almost starved to death. I was worried about if Kylan had enough milk. Charles thought something was wrong why we had not left. CJ even called me around two thirty. I see everyone else is used to my schedule now. So, we did not make it to Lumberton until five thirty. Yes, I am tired but today is my 'high' day because of the chemo. I am up at one thirty-two in the morning typing this journal entry. I'm getting ready to go to bed. The doctors say I am doing great and the myeloma is decreasing.

## *August 18, 2009*

I felt good on yesterday and spent today in the emergency room at Southeastern Regional Medical Center. Mondays and Tuesdays are days when I am suppose to drink plenty of fluids because of the chemo taken on Mondays. I guess I did not drink enough. I had the worst headache and stomach pain ever. I thought I was leaving this earth. When I finally made contact with Duke, I was throwing up like crazy. They could not understand me over the phone. CJ had to grab the phone and talk to them because I could not stop throwing up.

They were asking him if he was old enough to drive me to the hospital. (I wish!) Well, luckily, my mother-in-law had just came home so she took me. Duke called the hospital to let them know to expect me. When we got to the hospital, I could feel myself having to throw up again. I went to the bathroom. I fell to the floor. I was constantly throwing up. I could not lift myself up off the floor. They kept calling my name. All I can remember is my mother-in-law and a nurse coming in the bathroom and picking me up off the floor and placing me in a wheelchair and whisking me away in a room.

They took blood and ran x-rays on my chest and abdomen and hooked me up to some fluids to get me hydrated. The final verdict was that my electrolytes were out of whack and I was dehydrated. After being given hours of fluids, they sent me home. I am here now watching my beautiful niece while my mother-in-law and sister-in-law go to Lowe's.

Today was the first teacher workday for the 2009-2010 academic school year. If I were working, I would have been reporting to my new school—Lumberton Senior High School as the Digital Communications teacher. I will not be reporting now since I have been placed on short term disability for, at least, the remainder of the school year.

## *August 21, 2009*

Well, it is about one thirty in the morning and I am at home right now watching Lifetime with my sister, Venita—after fighting her about taking my medicine. I took it. Today was okay. Guess my blood count was fine. They immediately sent me to the treatment room and hooked up my IV. That was a good sign. Still had to wait an hour for the blood report. The only real problem was that my potassium was low AGAIN.

Yes, I am still eating my bananas and taking my potassium pills. They have just increased my dosage from ten mg to twenty mg (More darn horse pills to take. Those jokers are huge!) They had to give me some additional potassium through the IV. I'm leaving later and later from Duke it seems. We left about two pm today.

In running the potassium through the IV, they ran it very fast and it burned my veins (OUCH!) so they had to stop and run it again slowly. I know I'm ready to leave, but they did not have to rush the fluids through the body.

I'm noticing that I have been getting very weak and my energy level is decreasing somewhat. They told me to expect this. I did not expect it this quickly (No, not for the energizer bunny!) I asked Charles this morning if I had to go. I just didn't feel like getting up and out of the bed.

I am so weak! I have been thrown off schedule also because of Tuesday's episode. I'm starting to get tired of all of this! I'm ready to hang in the towel!

## *August 24, 2009*

Today is day eight of cycle two. Needless to say, the chemo is taking a toll on me physically and emotionally. I'm still okay though. At times, my energy level is decreasing. I'm having good days and bad days. It's all good. I had no problem getting chemo today other than them giving it to me at twelve noon. Normally, I had been leaving at twelve noon. They spoiled me in Cycle one.

Duke informed me that Tuesday's episode came from a virus. The hydration was a result of catching a virus. Yes, I knew I was doing what I was supposed to be doing. They still told me to watch what I eat—(i.e. buffet is OUT! Oh, take me away—I'm small, but y'all know I can eat!!!) What will I do? She said I need to avoid buffet, for example, because I do not know how long the food has been out nor who has handled the food, etc. My white blood count is already low which makes me less able to fight off any infection. Makes sense when you think about it. {Do I have to avoid buffet though?}

So, we left about twelve forty-five to come back just in time for CJ's Open House and then Michael's Open House and then my PTA meeting (Vice-President) at Michael's school. Yes, school is tomorrow. Yellow buses, here they come!!!

CJ and Michael will be at school. Kylan (Baby Girl) left on Sunday to go back to Columbia. It will just be me and 'Snoop', my yorkie. I'm about to go to bed. I wish all of my NC teachers a great first day tomorrow.

I am feeling out of place. I have never *NOT* been busy. [Is that proper English?] This is going to be extremely difficult. The doctor has me on short-term disability for a year. Well, y'all know me. Even my former principal said that if I continue like I am now, I'll be back sooner. I confirmed that. If you ask me, I should be back January/ February which is the beginning of second semester. That is putting it at the extreme end, if I have to complete all eight three-week cycles. I have to do at least four cycles. At this point, they are not exactly sure how many cycles I will have to do. I am re-evaluated (for lack of a better terminology) at the end of each cycle. Then I have to have the bone marrow stem cell transplant where I will be living in an apartment for about thirty-sixty days at Duke because I will have to be at the hospital every day versus the two days a week that I am currently doing.

## *August 27, 2009*

Today is day eleven of cycle two. Today was a good day. Left Lumberton early anticipating traffic in Raleigh/Durham since school began on Tuesday. We had no problems. Arrived thirty minutes early. They immediately took my blood work and hooked me up to my anti-nausea medicine. That was a good sign. The hour wait did not seem like an hour.

My blood work was okay. They gave me my chemo. All is well. I'm feeling okay. The nurse practitioner asked a favor of me while I was leveling off. I told her sure and then asked what it was. There was a lady who just began treatment this week. Our cases are so similar. We are around the same age (five year difference). I have two boys. She has three boys. We both have Myeloma, "the elderly disease", even though she has a different form of Myeloma. She is from the Triad area—she has about an hour drive. We both believe in God.

Well, I was asked if I could just talk to her to just let her know what to expect [Me, man, *I* don't even know what to expect? How can I talk to someone?] We talked for a while. You know, I mentioned sometime ago (or maybe several times even) that sometimes things happen not for us, but for someone else. I did not think about that then but as I sit here and write in this journal, I reflect on my own words.

I began walking toward her not knowing what to say to this perfect stranger, nor how she would take the information that I did give her. But I was obedient and I feel like I was the one who walked away feeling so much better having had the conversation.

That conversation was for me. I wonder how would I have felt if I said no? How would she have felt?

Debbie, I hope you got a chance to read this and browse through my website and you can begin your own, as we talked about. I hope that I only gave you an ounce of the joy you gave me. I feel a very close bond with you. I can't really explain it. I'm sure that you know what I mean. I know that this journal entry seems really weird and unusual to everyone else. But this was for **Debbie**—thanks for the bond. I'm there for you for whatever (and I'll be honest and say that I don't what 'whatever' may be). Just know that you got someone with you in your corner that truly understands.

## *August 30, 2009*

I went to church today and found out that the Missionary Department at my church is having a benefit singing program for me on October 4, 2009. Wow! I was totally unaware. That is Charles and Michael's birthday. They will also host a Cancer Benefit Cake Raffle. I just wanted to invite everyone to the program. My church is Oak Grove Missionary Baptist Church located at 2060 Turkey Branch Road in Fairmont, North Carolina. I did not see a time mentioned but I will find out and let everyone know. Words cannot express how I felt when I found out about this. To know that your church members think of you that much to have such a program is just unbelievable.

## *September 8, 2009*

Things are okay. I did not have to have chemo last Thursday (Days sixteen through twenty-one are resting days). I did not go on yesterday because it was a holiday (Labor Day). So, I am not on chemo this week. Praise be to God!

Now, next week, we have to see if I will be "good" as I was this past week. Monday, I will practically be at Duke all day. I have to arrive at eight am for my regular lab work. Be shuttled from the Bone Marrow Clinic to the main hospital for surgery.

I will have a Central Venuous Catheter (CVC) Placement done at ten am. This is where they will place a "mediport" on my right side kinda right below my collar bone. CVCs are used to give long-term medicine treatment for cancer. This will be an implanted port placed under my skin.

This will be where I will be stuck at from now on. I knew I would have to get this, but did not know when. I do not mind because the needles are killing my arms. My arms are making me look like a crackhead. I know I look like a pure "junkie".

The surgery will take so long and then I will have the recovery period and then I will be transported back to the Bone Marrow Clinic for my chemo, I pray. You know, that's if my blood count is okay. So, Monday will be an all day thing. Pray for me! Y'all know I don't do blood and needles anyway. This whole experience has been something for me; having to get stuck twice a week. I'll be honest and say that I am glad for the break this week.

The benefit singing program that my church is having for me is going to be at three thirty pm on October 4, 2009. Previously, I did not know the time. You know, my body must be used to the schedule even though I did not have my chemo on yesterday. I say that because Mondays and Tuesdays are my high days (Having the 'Decadron'—did I spell that right?) and Wednesdays are my down days (I sleep all day because my body is coming down off the high). But, I literally did not sleep all night last night. I feel okay so far though.

I'm being me trying to stay busy around the house. I am somewhat restricted by the doctor about going out alot in the midst of crowds. Since my white blood count is low, my body cannot fight off infections.

Right now I have an awful ear infection. It's very painful. I can't even hear out of my left ear. They prescribed me some antibiotics that I have to take for seven days. This began last Friday. Even though I have a terrible ear infection, it all went away (well in my mind) this weekend as I watched my beautiful niece, Kylan (Baby Girl). But she's gone and the boys are at school, Charles is at work, . . . it's just me and Snoop again as usual. Awww, now my ear hurts again.

## *September 15, 2009*

Today is day one of cycle three. It has been a very long day. I left home at five am and returned at five thirty pm. My appointment time started out at eight am at the Bone Marrow Clinic for lab work.

They wanted the labwork to get checked first before the rest of my dreaded day began.

Lab work was okay. The phlebotomist chuckled and said that this would be my last prick in my arm. I was shuttled to the main hospital for my surgery. Everyone there was so wonderful. I see why Duke is the medical research place in NC. Anyway, the doctor met with Charles and myself into a little room to explain the procedure step by step. They prepped me up. You talk about scared. Yes, I was scared. I cried like a baby after the doctor left telling me everything. I mean I boo-hooed. I have not had any major surgery other than two caesarian sections and a d and c. I'm scared.

It can be scary when you are told that you are going to get cut here and cut there and have this contraption placed in your body. You hear all of the side effects and all this stuff.

Can you believe that they did not give me any anesthesia? They gave me a sedation medicine. Okayyy, what's that? They said that this sedation medicine would make me comfortable but I would still have all five of my senses. Boy, did I. I do not remember the cutting nor the burning numbing medicine which the nurse told me is the same burning numbing medicine that they used for my bone marrow biopsies. (yes, it burns awful!) They had to cut through my neck to place the tube to connect to my lungs or something and then cut me to place the catheter and then connect the tube to the catheter. There is a nurse who monitors me constantly throughout the surgery—checking my pulse, oxygen, blood pressure, etc. I do remember feeling them pulling tubes. I guess I was comfortable because I fell asleep for a majority of the surgery. I woke up off and on.

They said that with the sedation medicine that I would not remember anything as far as what they said to me during the procedure and afterwards. (They don't know me!) I remembered it all! This is why they say someone must be with you. No exceptions! They have to sign off on the paperwork and everything. I actually saw them turn a gentleman away because he had no one with him. This stuff is serious! I was in recovery for two hours.

Earlier that day, we talked with the boys' godfather who told us about a fourteen or fifteen year old girl who got shot at the bus stop in his neighborhood this morning. Well, there was a lady who was also in recovery (she was there with her husband who had some type of surgery) who we overheard mentioning this same incident. Well, she happened to walk by and Charles asked her if she was from Charlotte (I was sleep at the time but still had those senses going on). We discussed our relationship with Charlotte and how we are in Lumberton now. She mentioned her church in Abbottsburg (I think I spelled it right). Anyway, we found out that we have some friends in common in Bladenboro, NC—The Wrights. Small world. We had a great conversation. You know, Charles does not meet any strangers. That's where Michael gets his personality and charisma from. She told us how she thoroughly enjoyed talking with us. We enjoyed it too! Most of all, we both needed it. Thanks, Ms. Mary!

After recovery, I was shuttled back to the Bone Marrow Clinic for my chemo. So now, I have a POWER PORT—implantable port. From this time forward, I just get a needle placed in the port. They said this is a top-of-the-line port (God's people only get the best!). I must carry this identification card, key ring and bracelet to inform any medical professional that I have this type of port. If I am ever having any type of procedure done which requires an IV, I just show them my card. It tells them where my port is so I will get stuck in the correct place. My port is good for both IV therapy treatments and power-injected Contrast-Enhanced Computer Tomography (CECT) scans. Y'all know that I copied that from the card.

Of course, now I am really on lock down. You talk about tired. Yes, I am beat down. I cannot do anything but rest for real. I have been doing just that. I'm not resisting at all. Believe it or not!! I purposely did alot last week during my week off because I knew after this, I would really be limited. Last week, I re-arranged my home office, re-arranged Michael's closet (gathered old clothes-size 8 that he is no longer wearing to pass on to the foster boy who is wearing size 8) and re-arranged CJ's room (gathered clothes too small for him to place in Michael's room). My deadline was to have everything completed by Sunday and I did just that. I am happy.

I will formulate a schedule for the boys to do things around the house, which they basically already do. The schedule I guess will be for me. You know how detailed I am.

Grandma was sent to the hospital this morning about nine forty-five am. Still having breathing problems, coupled with other issues. I am so not worried about me. I worry everyday about her. Charles said that we will go up there this weekend. I love my Grandma!!!! Please pray for her—Macie Barber in Baltimore, MD. (there's only one like her!) Not only her, pray for my mother who is taking care of her—Macie Alexander. My mom's patience is wearing down and she is a very patient person. I get my patience from her. Just pray for her and for added strength. I know she wants to be here with me.

My mother-in-law is here with me. My sister-in-law will be here with me the rest of the week until we leave for home on Friday.

## *September 18, 2009*

Yesterday (day four of cycle three) was fine. It was different. This was the first time using the portable catheter/port. I guess this was better because they did not have to stick me in the arm anymore. I messed up wearing the wrong type of shirt. I wore a T-shirt. I should have worn a button-up shirt or a low cut shirt which would have made it easier for them to access the port. They told me that but I guess I got too much going on to remember. I did not write that down.

They had to remove the bandages. Then they have some type of tool where they use alcohol on the tip and rub the area where the catheter is. Once the alcohol cools, they get something that they spray on me and gets extremely cold. At this point, it's numbing the area. Once the area is numb, they put the needle in my skin through the catheter. You know I always wondered how that was going to work, as far as them sticking a needle in me.

We also encountered another dilemma, . . . the needle was too long that they used for me. This caused the needle to not go all the way in. They had to put alot of tape around the needle area to my skin to keep it stuck in the port. At least now they made a note in my file of the needle size they will have to use later. C'mon, you can look at me and see how small I am. Stevie Wonder could see that I would need a small needle. This was my first time so it was a learning experience all the way around. Everything went okay after that.

Today is a different story though. Today is just a sluggish day. I have no energy whatsoever. After I got up at six to get the boys on the bus, I slept until around noon or one. Got up and washed which is still difficult because it still hurts to raise/move this right arm (where Monday's surgery was done). Kylan and my sister-in-law came from Columbia. I must be out of it because I do not have the energy to play and be with her like I normally would.

I feel so drained today and tired and I haven't even done anything. Let me lay back down. I can tell that things are going a different way. I'm just not used to not having no energy.

## *September 21, 2009*

I was only at Duke an hour today. Why? Well, my count was low. Way low. Lower than before. Eight hundred to be exact. Like before you may remember, it has to be at least a thousand for me to take my chemo. Before it was nine hundred and they sent home for the rest of that week. They did tell me this time to come back on Thursday and we will see what happens.

I did not go home to visit Grandma this past weekend. I am already not supposed to be around anyone sick because I am so open to infection. She's still in the hospital so I would be surrounded by sick people. So, I was home the weekend which was good. My husband and my youngest son had two singing engagements at our church—one on Saturday (Big Six of Robeson County) and one on Sunday (Homecoming). Boy, did they sing! I can't wait to get copies of the programs so I can mail them to Grandma.

## *September 30, 2009*

I know it's not my regular updating day—then again, I could do this everyday if I wanted to, but don't want to bore you guys with daily journal writings. Anyway, I just want to tell my friend, Terry, thanks so much for the laugh. All "80 lbs of me" enjoyed reading it. (Boy, you know how to bring it, don't you! That's what I'm talking about!). I am sitting here now wondering how did we, CDFs [Career Development Facilitators], get anything done in our business meetings with you clowning around.

Terry Jackson, you are the bomb! I miss you guys too. I got my Robeson County *CareerReady* newsletter today. Looks great! Oh, by the way, for those wondering about the growth in my ear. Don't worry! It's an inside joke. You see, at our Robeson County **CareerReady** Partnership meetings, our chairperson, Jon would always pick with me.

He would tell me that something is growing in my ear and it is blinking blue. He always suggested that I make an appointment with the hospital because they could remove this growth in my ear. IT WAS MY BLUETOOTH!!!

We always got a chuckle out of it!! Get it? Okay, if you didn't laugh, that's fine. Like I said, it was an inside joke. You had to be there to hear it and to hear it from Jon. I do miss my co-workers and I am still waiting on that lunch date. It's not like I'm doing anything but going to chemo twice a week. You all let me know what date is right with you guys. (Keep the laughter coming!) Have a great night! Gotta get ready and hope my count is up enough to have chemo. As much as I have been laughing tonight maybe it will be.

## September 24, 2009

I got my chemo today. Just my IV chemo. Everything went well today. Seems as if someone is always drawn to me. People just come and sit (uninvited) and have a conversation. Today, an older gentleman named David came and just had a conversation with me. He and his wife are from Virginia. His wife, Julia, also has Multiple Myeloma. He discussed different things that she was experiencing. I shared my experiences. We discussed family and job issues. We just talked about life. He said he was very happy to have talked to me.

Julia was at the stem cell transplant process right now. Everyone always says how I look so good and am so young to have Myeloma. I experienced the same thing on last Thursday. A woman came out of the bathroom (which was right in front of my treatment area) and looked at me and said 'I know that YOU don't have Multiple Myeloma'. I shook my head yes and she just walked away in awe.

I did get a spanking because I am out too much. I made mention that I went to PTA at both of my boys' schools. I was scolded because of how schools are full of viruses and flus. My doctor stated that I MUST stay in. My immune system is very, very low. At one time in the beginning, I did stay in for a while. I went out one time and thought that I was alright. So, I kept going out like normal. She stated that I MUST avoid crowds of people. I guess I must obey what they tell me. Now, I'm debating whether or not to attend CJ's football game tonight. I always support my boys.

## *September 26, 2009*

I did go to CJ's football game on Thursday and boy, was it a great game. They won against Princeton High School. (Fourteen to six) I love football. I had alot of fun. Guess I hollered and cheered too much. I went home with a terrible headache.

Thought I could sleep it off. I woke up Friday morning to an even worse headache. My temp was 99.9 so I called Duke and I had to take Tylenol Extra Strength. Well, I had two packed away. Wish she had said, Tylenol PM. That puts you in a coma. It knocks you out!

I took it at nine and she said around two, I should be feeling okay. And I was. My temp gradually decreased. I was still pretty weak. Grandma came out of the hospital and I really had to see her. So, Charles packed us up and 95 Northbound we were headed. I had to settle my emotional side and really see and be with her and hold her hand. I just had to! That's why I said, I will be better after this. We'll be leaving sometime in the morning heading back to Lumberton.

## *October 6, 2009*

Let me first back track and discuss last week—why there were no journal updates. Well, on my day fifteen of each cycle, the doctor at Duke made it somewhat convenient for me in that I just go to the Gibson Cancer Center here in Lumberton to get my bloodwork drawn and they would fax the report to Duke and Duke would call me back to confirm whether or not I can take my oral chemo. We had done this twice so far and it had worked good—definitely saves on the driving. You see, on day fifteen, I only have my oral chemos and not the IV so they say there was no need to drive to Duke just to take all those pills when I can take them at home. Makes sense.

Last week, both of my wonderful nurse practitioners were out (Catherine and Angela), my two angels. My bloodwork got faxed a little after twelve on Monday but no one ever received it until

Tuesday afternoon. I just knew I was in the clear for not having to take that chemo. Then when I got the call from Patty so late in the afternoon on Tuesday, I was concerned. I did not tell her, but I did not want to take it because I knew that it would throw the rest of my weekly schedule off. So I was on my high on Tuesday and Wednesday and wanted to sleep on Thursday, but could not because I was trying to tidy up the house since we were expecting company/family for the weekend (Benefit singing at my church).

I could not get my days right because I was going by how my body felt. It just was not a good week for me. At least, not until Friday night, my dad was first to arrive from home (Baltimore). I always re-emphasize that Baltimore is my home because so many people think that Charlotte is my home. That is my second home.

At this point, we had to tell Edie because Mommie wanted to come and she needed to see if Edie would be able to watch Grandma. For me, it was extremely difficult to tell those whom I am very close with. Edie was one of those individuals. It has been months and we have not told her. It was easy to refer people to the website, let them read it and then you can come and talk to me about it or not. Some people, even after knowing, still said that they did not know what to say or how to approach me. I always tell everyone "Dee is still Dee".

Well, Mommie apparently could not tell Edie either. I would always ask her if she told Edie. I told her to give Edie the website and let her read it. Eventually, Edie read the website and cried like everyone else did. Later she blessed me out for not telling her earlier. She did that out of love. That just comes with our relationship. I really should have told her. She, like me, began researching the disease. Edie was able to take off that Monday so Mommie was able to come to North Carolina Saturday morning. She could not find anyone to keep Grandma on that Friday.

Others came in from Charlotte, NC, Lancaster, SC and Rock Hill, SC also. A great time was had by all. For those who don't know, Charles is the cook of the family and loves to play host. He and Michael had a singing engagement at Greenville Church on Saturday night but afterwards, he came home and we cooked out. We had ribs, fish, and cole slaw. Everyone stayed up until five or six in the morning playing cards, eating, watching TV and just having fun. People were coming to the house at two in the morning like it was two in the afternoon. We had a blast!

Sunday was the Benefit Singing Program sponsored by the Missionary Department at my church. It was awesome! I never had such a great time. If you weren't there, you missed a treat. The church was packed and there were many people who were unable to come due to prior engagements. I could imagine how the church would have been had everyone came. As we drove up, I was shocked to see one of my fellow co-workers, Mr. Matthew Locklear (Electrical Trades Instructor) and my CTE Director, Mr. Merle Summers, drive in also. As I walked in the church, I immediately cried when I saw my former co-workers and their families from Robeson Community College and the Robeson County Career Center. I had to go in the bathroom and get myself together. It was just too overwhelming!

The groups in attendance were my church choir (Oak Grove Mass Choir), Mr. Delano Townsend and the Voices of Triumph, Mrs. Teresa Hunt, Min. Robert Jones and Company, David Spencer and Dynamic Production, True Committed (Kingstree, SC), Mt. Pilar, the Bostic Family, and Soldiers for Christ (Charlotte, NC). The two who really made me lose my composure were Bryanna Grice. She is no more than four years old but she gave the ABC's of having Victory in Jesus. She sung through each alphabet without reading anything. She was wonderful! And then there were the Sisters of Faith, a group formulated by my five cousins. When my cousin's daughter sung the second song, I just lost it.

I'm nothing but a ball of water anyway. If I don't remember anything else, all I can see is her singing this song. This cousin has always sung with the group, but had never sung a solo, and she was always low key. All of a sudden, they said that she was going to dedicate a song to me. I am sure that they did not know that this was one of my favorite songs. My only problem was she just did not sing it long enough. Let me just share the words with you. It's called "Encourage Yourself" by Donald Lawrence and the Tri-City Singers.

**VERSE 1:**

*Sometimes you have to encourage yourself*
*Sometimes you have to speak victory during the test*

*And no matter how you feel*
*Speak the word and you will be healed*
*Speak over yourself*
*Encourage yourself in the Lord*

**VERSE 2:**

*Sometimes you have to speak the word over yourself*
*Depression is all around you but God is present help*
*The enemy created walls*
*But remember giants, they do fall,*
*Speak over yourself*
*Encourage yourself in the Lord.*

**BRIDGE:**

*As I minister to you, I minister to myself,*
*Life can hurt you so,*
*'til you feel there's nothing left*
*(No matter how you feel)*
*(Speak the word and you will be healed)*

Now, my cousin did not sing verse two or the bridge, but she sung that verse one enough that you felt it. It had been a while since I had heard that song. You know sometimes, we have to be reminded of things. There are no words that can describe what I felt.

It was good to see those who came out. I'll be honest. I was so in and out, and off and on that I did not see everyone. So, if I did not see you (and even if I did see you), please hit me up on the guestbook and let me know how you enjoyed the program. You know, it was not all about the money. It was about coming to support and to get a blessing. Some told me that they did not come because they did not have any money to give. It was not about that! That was probably the intention of the Missionary Department. Just as in the words of that song, [and the Bishop (whom I do not know—he was not a member of our church) even said yesterday], when you come to bless someone else, you will receive a blessing.

The mother of young Bryanna Grice, also said that yes, they were honoring me that day but tomorrow it may be your day. We do not know from day to day. So much is going on in the world on a daily basis. The next hour is not promised to anyone. None of us are so good that God needs us. We need him!

The King James version says (Proverbs 18:24) that a "man that has friends must show himself friendly and there is a friend that sticks closer than a brother." I was truly humbled at the number of people who came and those who came. Some people came and I don't even know them. Ain't that something? (y'all know I'm not working so I'm not using correct English.) That's what it's all about. We are to help everyone, whether we know them or not.

Charles was a little hurt that certain people/family members did not show up. Me, it did not bother me because those who were destined to be there were there and God was going to bless them. That day was already made out to be as it was. My steps were ordered by the Lord long before Schuyler and Macie ever even knew they were going to have a daughter named Demetria Michele Alexander (Grissett).

(I told my mom this was going to be a long journal entry.) But anyway, to my great news. You know, we had this great singing Sunday and I pray that everyone else was encouraged and had a good time. I felt that they did. During the service, the Bishop asked if I were in the church and he asked me to come out into the aisle. He told people that if you love her (meaning me), just run to her and hug her. Different people came and prayed over me and hugged me. Everyone just came all at the same time. The Spirit of God was all in that place. I truly felt His awesome power like never before.

Well, Monday was day one of cycle four. You know in the beginning, I said I did not know how many cycles of chemo I would have. The max is eight. The minimum is four. At the beginning of each cycle there is a restaging process to see if you have to continue chemo.

I'm getting ready to get scientific, so bear with me. At each restaging process, they are looking at what is called the IG KAPPA. Mine have been the following:

On 6/17/09, it was 332.00
On 7/9/09, it was 320.00

On 8/10/09, it was 1.39
On 9/14/09, it was 0.26

In less than a month, it dropped down twelve (from 332 to 320). Then in the next month, it dropped down three hundred nineteen. Wow!!!! Then in the next month it drops down a little less than one and a half. What does this mean? I guess that the cancer has gone into remission. Hallelujah!!!!!!!!!!!!! Okay, you know I had to look up the straight definition of remission. I have always heard the word but never understood the full meaning. Remission is that point in time when the disease starts subsiding in terms of symptoms and intensity. The period of remission may go on only for a short time or it may prolong for many months or even years.

So, I will still have to complete my cycle four this month. They will restage me on day one of cycle five which will be October 26. I will have to do the 24 hour urine thing again and have another dreaded bone marrow biopsy. (Ouch, those hurt!)

If my IG KAPPA remain the same, they said that I am ready for stem cell transplant which means that I will be living in an apartment at Duke. I will have to go to the hospital all day every day instead of the twice a week deal. So, we will be looking at that the next couple of weeks as well as seeing if they will use my own stem cells or utilizing a donor.

I guess that shoots down my plans for wanting to spend Thanksgiving with Grandma. They say I will be there for about seven to eight weeks. I'm gonna miss my boys. They will be allowed to come and see me on the weekends as long as they are not sick at the time. They are very strict on that.

I would be selfish if I did not share my praise report. See, I told y'all that God was going to work and he is still working. He's not done yet. And I know that he has done something for someone else. I mean, I don't know specifically, but I know, because I told y'all this journey was not just for me. Okay, I need to get up and shower and wash clothes or something, it's a high day . . .

I love all of you. To the Missionary Department and the entire Oak Grove Missionary Baptist Church family, you know that you are all family to me! Mommie and Daddy, thanks for making the long trip down. I know that you guys would not have it any other way.

I know that Grandma would have been there had she been strong enough and if she knew. Thank you to all of the groups and singers who were on program. I wanted to send each of you a thank you card and Rev. Mae Love told me to not worry about that.

Robeson Community College, Robeson County Career Center, Public Schools of Robeson County—you guys are the greatest! Words cannot express how you make me feel! To all of my family members by blood and marriage (you are too many to name)—THANK YOU EVERYONE!!! I feel so bad because today was Charles and Michael's birthday and I was not able to get them anything. Everyone has me under the camera all the time—I am never by myself. I never had a chance to get them anything.

The monetary blessing was truly needed, but I was more concerned and happy with your presence—I hope that you got a blessing. I guess if I was not crying so much yesterday, I could have said all of this to everyone at the program. I was just choked up! Yeah, me! Everyone have a blessed day and life is short! Don't forget to tell someone that you love them, if you really do! Be true to yourself!

## *October 11, 2009*

Thursday was an okay day. Got to Duke early around nine thirty am. Was able to get my chemo. It was an extremely long wait though. They can tell that my energy level is down because Thursday and Monday was the first week that I have gone to Duke and raised up the recliner and slept for a minimum of an hour. I am always in a recliner or bed but I never sleep. I am always doing something. My red blood cell count has been very low so I am more tired than usual.

Got out at two pm. Good timing! Thanks Aunt Ree for always going with me every Thursday since the beginning! Well, I felt alright and I went to CJ's football game. This was a big game: South Robeson versus Fairmont; the two rival high schools. Aunt Ree even went. The boys did not play as well as they have been. I don't know what was wrong with them tonight. We lost. The score was twenty-eight to zero.

Well, from four o'clock Friday morning until around ten am, I had diarrhea BAD! The doctor said either I caught a bug (from being outside like I was) or had a bad reaction from the chemo the day before. Had hot and cold chills, my temp did not get above 99 degrees and was just very, very weak.

Duke told me to take some Imodium and to keep drinking plenty of fluids because they knew that I got/was getting dehydrated. So, I had to drink eight glasses of some type of fluid and eat bland foods. Felt a little alright on Saturday afternoon and I was okay today to go to church—until someone said something to me that really "pissed me off" to put it plainly. And it took me a lot to go to church this morning. After that incident, I wonder if I should go back. That was my initial reaction. I can't let somebody else make me to go to hell.

My blood pressure is up right now. I even broke the handle on my Kirby vacuum cleaner of sixteen years cleaning up. Cleaning up is therapeutic for me so I thought I could vacuum it away. I got more upset. Some of you (who don't know me very well) are saying "Is this Dee talking like this?" Dee is human, okay? When you push one of Dee's buttons, she just pops like a fire cracker. And that's probably anybody.

Got this cancer going on. My grandmother was just rushed to the hospital on Tuesday and she is all that has been on my mind since Tuesday. If I were not sick on Friday, I would have been home. Then I would not have been at church on Sunday to get the "talk" that I had with someone.

And I was so excited to share with you guys news that I got on Tuesday. I heard so many praise reports from people who attended Sunday's service, you would not even believe—prayers have been answered. Some prayed for a job, some lost weight, some got financial blessings, some got a new revelation of God, and the list can go on and on. It was great to hear how everybody was touched through the ministry of the Missionary Department.

On Tuesday, I heard all of these great things, had some former co-workers to come to the house and eat lunch with me and I am glad that they were with me because that's when I got a call about Grandma. She was rushed to St. Agnes Hospital again. My news was going up and down. One day I got good news then I got bad news and then I got good news, up and down, touch and go. Her heart rate was racing. From that Tuesday to the following Monday, things just did not even feel right because Grandma would always tell everybody how her "Michael" calls her everyday. She would often tell Mommie to call me and let me know that she [Grandma] was waiting for my call. It felt strange to not talk to Grandma. I have always talked to her everyday. Two to three times a day nearly. For over twenty years now.

She is not doing well. She's hanging in there and we thank God for that! Get sick on Friday and disgusted on Sunday. You know it takes alot for me to get disgusted but I am one that has to say what I feel and get it off my chest and I'm through with it.

Let me take my blood pressure pill with all of my other pills. I'm gonna try to get back on track on tomorrow after treatment.

## *October 12, 2009*

Yesterday was my venting day. That had nothing to do with my treatment. Like I told someone today—sometimes people place you on a pedestal like you do no wrong [granted this is their perception of you] and when something happens proving that you are human, oh my God, put it on the front page of the Robesonian (local newspaper) will you. They want to blow everything (which was nothing) up!

Duke went well today. Charles went with me. I think this was so he could get information on our next steps as we phase into transplant. I forgot my chemo pills. I took those dreaded pills once I got home. Truth be told, I'm really tired of taking them now. Charles told me that we don't have long to go and that I need to hang in there. He has been my encourager and strength throughout this entire process from day one. I love my "Pookie"!!! He's been there to encourage me during the nights when I just brake out crying for no reason. I cry because I'm upset that I have cancer. I cry because I can't do and be there for Grandma like I want to and need to. I cry because I feel like God has left me. Sometimes I feel so alone. And I know I'm not.

I have two more weeks to take these pills, I think. On Oct. 26 which will be day one of cycle five, I will get re-staged meaning I will have another bone marrow biopsy (Ooooouch!—Not again!), EKG, Chest X-ray, and all of those other tests as before. They explained to me that if my IG KAPPA is still the same, then we will go to the transplant stage. I will have to have surgery again to have the current catheter port removed and another type of catheter port will be placed in me to be used strictly for transplant. I will be given a different type of chemo (high dose) that will make me lose all of my hair. [My mom reminded me that I have been bald headed before—when I was born]

They will remove my stem cells and freeze them. Throughout this time, I have had a low immune system. At that time, I will have NO immune system at all because all of my cells will be depleted. This of course is why I will be at Duke—living in an apartment in Durham. They have close monitoring that they must do for safety and insurance reasons. They will give me another high dose chemo to finally kill off the Myeloma. Then the transplant will begin as they replace my cells and during this time, my body is expected to reproduce the white blood cells in the bone marrow [normal functionality] to build up my immune system.

I think I just gave you the highlights. There's alot more going on in between all of that stuff. Just pray for me. And pray for my Grandma—Macie Barber in Baltimore, MD. She is not doing well. I'm trying to go and see her. I really need to see her! I was trying to wait until Thanksgiving. Well now, I'll be on lock down for November and December so there goes Thanksgiving and Christmas holidays.

## *October 15, 2009*

Day eleven of cycle four. Went okay. Left a little later than normal (one o'clock pm). My count was pretty low. They had to get approval from higher up to say it was okay. They told me that I just need to be extremely careful—you know, wash hands all the time and the usual stuff.

I asked Mommie how come Grandma hasn't asked about me calling her or her talking to me. Well, Mommie informs me that she is no longer talking. This is very upsetting to me. I did not let my mother know how much this upset me. After we talked that night, I break out and cry. I know that no one lives forever, but I want my Grandma to stay with me as long as possible. God knows best though. Well, what do I do? Of course, we go home. I could not take it not being with her. We (Charles, myself and the boys) left Tuesday night to go home and arrived Wednesday morning. We spent all day Wednesday with Grandma in the hospital. We left Wednesday night driving back to North Carolina. We got back to Lumberton around two this morning. I did not want the boys to miss more than one day of school knowing that they would soon be missing much more. I will have chemo on Thursday.

Then I will pack up and I will be catching Amtrak heading back up the road (Yes, I will be wearing my mask on the train!) My train leaves at one in the morning. I will be coming back Sunday afternoon. Sorry, this journal entry is very short! All I can say is pray for me and my Grandma!

This was very difficult for me. Knowing that I am about to go through another stage and how I really want and need to be with Grandma is just overwhelming emotional for me to deal with right now. I told my mother that I prayed for Grandma to see her 77th birthday (December 30th). How things are looking now, I find it very hard to believe that she will see that. Grandma has so many issues going on—high blood pressure, rheumatoid arthritis, diabetes, kidneys are failing, congestive heart failure, she's not talking and now she refuses to eat anything. She has not eaten in about a week now. Her Advanced Health Care Directive stated that she be given no nutrition intravenously or otherwise. So, when you do not eat, you do not live. All she is being given is morphine for her pain from the rheumatoid arthritis. And that's it!

She went from the hospital to FutureCare (Hospice). At this point, all the doctors said they could do is give her meds to keep her comfortable. What the heck is *comfortable*? I am sitting here now at FutureCare. I am not comfortable. There is no internet which is good because it has allowed me to continue focusing on writing my book. I am just sitting here and I feel like I am watching her die. Oh God, this is the hardest thing. Daddy and Edie were also in the room. They went to the vending machines. I stayed in the room. I was told that she hadn't been talking in a week. All of a sudden, she looks up at me straight in the eyes, as I held her hand, and said, "What do you want me to do?" She said it so clear. She caught me off guard. As I held back the tears, I told her, "I just want you to be happy, Grandma."

Edie walked in right after I said what I said. I rushed to the bathroom and cried. Edie asked me what had happened and closed the door behind me. I'm thinking that she did not want Grandma to see or hear me crying. I came out and told her what was said. Edie replied that "she gets to you like that sometimes". I'm glad Daddy didn't see me. I was okay for a while. This was something to let me know that she was slowly but surely letting go. Hospice had been informing us of a lot of things to expect from her.

Of course, if I had my way, things would be different. She would be eating if I had to force it down her throat myself. I realize that we must honor her wishes which she has laid out in black and white. I'll be leaving on tomorrow morning (Sunday) because I have chemo again on Monday. But I will be off the rest of the week because it is days sixteen through twenty-one [resting days] of cycle four. I will be back. Just like I told my dad who just left; I feel better when I am here. He is very concerned about the travel and he knows how low my immune system is and does not want me to catch anything especially with the swine flu (H1N1) and other stuff going on. I assured him that I will be alright. God will take care of me.

I'm going to talk with my doctor on Monday to see how the situation with Grandma will affect my schedule for transplant. Plain and simple, I am just going to have to have a delay. I don't know how long it will be or even if it is allowed. It must happen. No question. I cannot function otherwise.

## October 18, 2009

It is October 18, 2009. It is day fifteen of cycle four and I am leaving on the train heading back to Lumberton. I have chemo tomorrow locally. That's a good thing. I will get my blood work drawn at the Gibson Cancer Center in Lumberton and they will fax my report to Duke and the nurse practitioner will call me to let me know whether or not I can take my oral chemo. I praise God that this will be my last time taking those dreaded pills. I am sick and tired of taking those pills!

When I talk with my nurse practitioner, I will discuss with her my proposed future schedule and my feelings and dilemma with Grandma. As I am riding back, I sit and think about a lot of things. These past four months have really given me a whole new perspective and outlook on every aspect of my life. There are so many things in life that people take for granted, myself included.

## *October 20, 2009*

You know from the previous entry, I went home again after Thursday's chemo. Got home Friday morning. Charles recommended that I get a one way ticket this time. He will get the boys out of school on Friday at twelve noon and they will drive up the road. I hope that he does not think that I will drive back with him on Sunday because if he does, and Grandma is still not right or I do not feel ready to go back, guess what? You got it, I'm not going back! And my doctor said I don't have to. I left Fayetteville twenty minutes late. Not too bad. I actually arrived on time in Baltimore at eight fifty pm. Too late to see Grandma though. Visiting hours are over at eight pm at FutureCare. I guess I will see her in the morning. Mommie and I spent some of the night cleaning the house up some. I am expecting a lot of company to go along with the many phone calls we have been receiving at the house with people checking up on Grandma.

Got up in the morning after Wednesday, my "down" day. Got a call at five in the morning asking where my son's wallet is because he needed money for his homecoming game. Then Mommie and I went through jewelry. We shredded bank statements from four, five and six years ago. We then headed to Rite-Aid to get some masks because I switched handbags. I brought a bigger suitcase which meant I left my masks at home.

We are here now with Grandma. Mommie informs me that Grandma did not respond at all on yesterday. She did not open her eyes nor move like before. As I have been with her today, she still does not respond.

In my heart though, I feel like something will happen this weekend when Grandma sees the boys. I have heard old people say that sometimes people are holding on until they see a certain person. I think that she is holding on until she sees her boys. She asked us about the boys Saturday—"Where are my boys?" Edie looked at me and I looked at Edie. We did not know what to say. We did not say anything. Grandma then went back into her zone. She threw us off because she had not been talking and then out of the blue, she asks that. That was just like before when she asks me out of the blue 'what did I want her to do?'

The simplest thing is just living from day to day. You never know if you, or your loved one, will live to see the next day, or the next hour. We all hope that we live. None of us hope to die. Or at least not before our time. But how do you know when your time is? Guess no one knows that either. That is why it pays to be ready at all times.

My husband is a truck driver. His job always has me on edge because when I hear of a terrible truck wreck I'm looking and have to ask myself, "Where is he at?" And now I'm dealing with this with Grandma. I know that no one lives forever, but I never thought that I would see Grandma in the situation she is in now. NEVER! I can remember telling Grandma that she was too stubborn to die. Out of her four sisters who are still living, she is the one who always traveled, is always physically fit, bowling, and exercising. She could run circles around me. She can't be *dying*. I am not ready for her to go. Don't she know that I need her—now more than ever.

I talked with Charles last night. I think he is having a worse time dealing with this than I am. I told him that I was finally coming to the realization that things are not looking good. I have prayed that God's will be done and that He gives me the strength to be able to accept His will, even if it is not what I want. He kept telling me to not say the things I was saying. I basically told him that it is just a matter of days and that I was thinking about coming back up on Monday or Tuesday after chemo.

He replied, "No, no, things are going to get better." Charles' grandmother passed away in March of this year. He reminded me how his grandmother was doing bad at one time and then got better. He tells me that Grandma will get better. I told him the difference was that his grandmother was eating. Grandma has not eaten in a week. She refuses to be given any nutrition or anything by mouth or intravenously. Her kidneys have failed. Her heart is slowly failing. All of her internal functions are shutting down. She is not responding.

No one can live forever by not eating. Being with Grandma all yesterday has helped me to realize and accept that she is not coming back to her physical home. Charles really got upset on the phone. But fact was fact.

When she was in the hospital a while back, she spoke about seeing my godfather who has been deceased. Later she asked the doctor if she saw the man dressed in white standing at her hospital door. No one was at the door. The doctor thought she was crazy. Literally. Yeah, Grandma is crazy alright, but not like Dr. Dang thought. She actually brought in a psychiatrist to talk to Grandma.

Like that was going to do something. Grandma worked as a Psychiatric Health Aide at University Hospital. They could not fool her. The psychiatrist probably left out feeling crazy.

I am slowly accepting the fact that Grandma is tired and God knows, I do not want her to be tired. I cannot stand to see her like I do. I have learned to appreciate those who I love and to tell them that I love them so there will be no question and no doubt. Sometimes people pass and you wonder 'Did they know that I love them?' Or sometimes they go with an animosity against a loved one. Life is too short for all of that. Especially now!

Growing up, I always heard 'Jesus is coming back'. And I truly believe and know that he is. I believe it now more so than ever. I can see the signs of the times more now than I ever have in my life. There are so many wars, fires, killings, etc. People need to have their life together before God takes them and it is too late!

I have always been a passive person. Easy-going. I go with the flow of the things until . . . . you press that button. Many people have never seen 'that' side of me. You may go through life and never see it [God bless you if you do not] and that means you have never done anything to me to 'press that button'. But I have also learned that you got to get stuff off of your chest and your mind. Lately, things that upset me, . . . I have just been getting off my chest and letting the people know right then and there., in a Godly and tactful manner. Why hold it in? That is probably how I was diagnosed with high blood pressure about four years ago. Holding stuff in.

Number one, I have too much going with me emotionally and physically to add on extra baggage. Secondly, the Bible says you should not go to bed mad. I have always been taught to do what the Bible says so hey, I'm not going to bed angry. So, I must let the person know what they did and how I feel about it.

Stayed with Grandma all day Friday until she was discharged late Friday night to Hospice at FutureCare Irvington. Spent Saturday morning with my dad and we went to see Grandma that afternoon and, of course, I stayed until they put us out that night. [Boy, are they strict with that!] Grandma was still the same. No eating. No movements. Just breathing. I did not want to go. I did not want anything to happen and I not be there. I left Sunday morning back on Amtrak. {I need to take stock in Amtrak, what do you think? How is the market for Amtrak? Anybody know?}

Yeah, that was a long train ride. Should have been in Fayetteville at three thirty pm. Got there at five pm. I guess what's important is that I got there.

Yesterday was day fifteen of cycle four. On my day fifteens, I go to the Gibson Cancer Center here locally and they draw my blood and fax the report to Duke and Duke will call me to say 'yea' or 'nay' if I can take my chemo. My appointment was bright and early at eight thirty am.

I spent the rest of the day washing clothes to repack again because I knew I was going to leave again on Tuesday. I got concerned because it was about three thirty and I had not heard from anyone at Duke regarding my bloodwork.

She eventually called and said my count was low; not as low as last week, but it was low. They had to get approval. Heaven knows, I dread taking those pills. I pray that this is the last time that I have to take them. I explained to her the situation that I am going through with Grandma. I told her that I was going home again and we do not really know how things are going to span out. She said the timing is great, because I am at the end of a cycle. But even if I wasn't, she said that they do provide leeways because sometimes things can happen that are out of your control. I fit that category. This was something that was out of my control.

She said she would keep my appointment for Monday, but that I will need to call her on Friday if I will need to change it. Because my body is very vulnerable, she told me to wash my hands all of the time [she should know by now, that I was already a clean freak] and to call her immediately if my temperature goes above 100.5° and she will prescribe me something up here.

Well, what can I say? I am worried about me, don't get me wrong, but I tell you what—my focus is on Grandma and my mommie. I love them both. I am learning to accept that she will not make it. Charles tells me that I should not talk like this about Grandma and he knows (like everybody else) how I feel about her.

I know that God is a miracle-worker but when you are not eating and request to not eat, c'mon . . . God gave us all common sense. Some use it more than others. When your internal functions are shutting down . . . . God is preparing me in his own way. Never in a million years would I have thought to see Grandma the way I see her. Never!!! Those of you who have been blessed to have known and met her, know what I am talking about.

Then I worry about my mommie. Both of us "only children". (Yeah, I had to brake the cycle!) It's hard!!! She wants to be here with me (her only baby) but she has to take care of her mother (her only mother)—that's biblical. She gotta do that. Everyday. All day. It's a strain on her.

Oh, speaking of her—she corrected me the weekend. You know, in my previous entry when I talked about my hair coming out and I'll be bald headed and I said that my mother said 'Oh, you've been bald headed before', I assumed that she meant when I was born, which I did have a few strands. I was not completely bald. (That's why Grandma called me 'TWEETY BIRD') but anyway, she recalled after I had CJ, I stopped taking my prenatal vitamins. I said oh well, I wasn't pregnant anymore, I did not need to take them. So I stopped and my hair broke off in the back. My hairdresser in Charlotte cut my entire head short and shaved the back where the hair would grow back evenly and it did. So, I corrected myself, Mommie. Even though I did not consider that situation because I was not completely bald. That was the first time my hair was cut and wasn't long anymore.

Pray for us. I almost feel like Job. I cannot put into words how I feel. I know that none of us will live forever. I know that we all have an expiration date. This process has showed me to not take little things for granted. There was a time when CJ would come plop his big behind (twice my size) on my lap and give me a hug and kiss, I would shy him away, 'Ok, son, you're too big for that!'. You gotta appreciate times like that. Walking down the street with Michael enjoying nature. You gotta enjoy times like that. Watching 'Drag

Racing' with Charles. You gotta enjoy times like that. Things like my 'Mom's Best Award', 'Mom's Greatest Award', things that the boys put time and effort into making. Little things. Those little things give you memories. Memories are embedded in you. You can't get rid of them. They are with you forever and I am glad about that.

Okay, I have completely gone off of journalizing my chemo treatment experiences. Just bear with me. Grandma is all that is on my mind right now. I need to pack. I'll be leaving Fayetteville at one pm. Everyone have a good rest of the week. And hey, if something doesn't go your way today, just brush it off like water on a duck. It will be alright. Grandma always told me to never complain. She always guaranteed me that there was someone else worse off than me who would love to trade places with me. I cannot imagine who would want to trade places with me right now!

## *October 22, 2009*

Everything is still the same. Grandma has not responded at all again. Today feels funny. I brought my laptop but did not use it at all while with Grandma. All I could do was just hold and rub her left arm. I stayed up until a little after midnight chatting with a friend on Facebook whom I have not seen or heard from in years. We grew up together at my church in Baltimore. She also resides in North Carolina. I eventually went to bed about twelve thirty in the morning.

Well, the phone rang at two. Oh boy. I woke up shaking. My mother answered the phone. She quickly went into the other bedroom. When I heard her say, "What time?" I knew. I began to cry to myself. I heard her repeat the time and say one forty-five. She came and told me that Grandma passed away at one forty-five am. We hugged each other and cried. I am so so so so glad that I was here with Mommie. I do not know what I would have done if she had found out and had been here by herself. Mommie called Edie and told her the news. I wanted to go to FutureCare to see her. Mommie did not think it was a good idea. We did not know what else to do so we went downstairs and began going through more paperwork that we had been going through all week long. Well, this time it was serious! We gathered together life insurance policies and just sat and drank hot tea watching "Without A Trace" marathon.

I waited until about five in the morning to call Charles to let him know. He and the boys were supposed to be leaving Lumberton around noon, but when I told him the news he said that they would leave as soon as he got back home from work which would be around nine. Before I had even told him what time everything had happened, he told me how he had been up since two a.m. and could not go back to sleep. He said he had the strangest feeling. He said that while he was on the road, something kept telling him to call me but he thought that I was sleep so he would not call.

He said he knows that he has not been in the family long (seventeen years—that's not long?), but he felt like he knew Grandma all his life. I could understand him. Grandma made everyone feel like that. If she knew you and liked you (or didn't like you), you were a part of her. Not many people can make you feel so much a part of them. I cannot think of anyone she did not like. Grandma loved everyone. Everyone loved her.

Charles said he was going to get the boys out of school as soon as he delivered his load. Charles was going to pick up Michael from school. My mother-in-law went to pick up CJ from school. He got in her car and asked her "Did my Grandma Macie pass away?" She tried to avoid answering the question. She asked him what made him say that. Charles wanted to tell the boys in his own way.

I was a little upset (Charles was a lot upset) to find out that one of my young cousins had text CJ with the news. First, this should have been left up to us to do. They did not know or care how CJ might have reacted. And he was at school when he got the text. After all, this was his very close great-grandmother. His *only* great-grandmother. What was he thinking? CJ could have lost it. I'm so glad he didn't. CJ always manages to keep it together. He gets that from his mom. Oh well, it's done now. We spent the rest of the day delivering the news—making calls and answering phone calls. I worked on writing the obituary.

## *October 23, 2009*

Please continue to keep me and my mom and my family in your prayers. God came and took his greatest angel from this earth, my grandmother, Macie Barber, at one forty-five this morning. We are happy because we know that she is no longer in pain but in peace!

Today was busy. We spent the day basically calling people. We were waiting for the funeral home director to call us but we called them and set up a two o'clock appointment. Vaughn Greene Funeral Home was wonderful! Mr. Greene dealt with us personally and that truly made a difference. Grandma loved them and how they performed services. But oh my goodness, we were there ALL day. We established a date and time for the viewing and funeral. We selected services and a casket. Grandma had everything laid out as far as what she wanted so everything was easy to do. I have never experienced anything like this. This is new to me; as far as, figuring out what to do when a loved one has passed away.

We got home late and Charles and the boys had met us at home. We were just busy making phone calls informing people of the arrangements or people were calling us offering condolences. We then tried to sleep. Mind you, we have not slept since two in the morning and it's late in the evening now. Boy, it has been a day!

## *October 25, 2009*

I wake up and it seems like I have just had a bad dream. Something is telling me that what I have been seeing has not been real. I am going to hear Grandma's voice in a minute. I sit up in the bed and I wait. And I wait. And I wait some more. Then I realize what has just happened and that Grandma is not coming back. I break down and just cry on the side of the bed. All I can think about is Grandma is no longer here with me. This cannot be real! God help me!!! Yeah, I know that she is in a better place. I know that she is no longer suffering. She is no longer in pain, but in peace. I know that I will see her again. I know all of this.

I just feel like my Grandma left me too soon! I was not ready for her to go! I wanted her to see her boys graduate from high school and go to college and see them get married and all that stuff. I wanted her to see Michael become that preacher/singer she always said he would be. I wanted her to see CJ graduate top of his class and attend college. Grandma has always been there for me for <u>everything</u>. What am I going to do now? I know that I have my mother but Grandma is Grandma. Charles just constantly hugs me. I feel the boys eventually coming in the room and surrounding and hugging me. Oh God, help me to be strong! I eventually get up and start to take my shower and begin writing in my CaringBridge journal. We have a two o'clock appointment today at the cemetery (Arbutus Memorial Park). I pray that we are not there all day like we were yesterday at the funeral home. I'm eating before I go this time.

I can remember when I was younger and Grandma was paying for her funeral stuff but I did not know at that time. I was too young to know what she was doing. I see these papers now and can recall that this is what she was doing back then. She wanted to be placed in a crypt and already had it paid for. The young lady took the *Certificate of Ownership* at Arbutus Memorial Park and then proceeded to show us how the service would be once we arrive from the church. She then showed us where the crypt was. It already had her name and birth year on it.

I called Duke to let them know what happened. I told my nurse practitioner that I was not sure at this point when I would return. She said that the latest that I could stretch my next appointment would be November 2nd.

## *October 27, 2009*

Me, my mother and Edie met with the clergy at the church today to develop the program. We knew for sure that we wanted the vocal choir to sign. We did not care about anything else. Singing was near and dear to Grandma's heart. She sang on several choirs but she really loved the vocal choir. We did not care about anything else. Everything else was customary at any funeral. We had to select songs and speakers for brief remarks. We then went to the funeral home to drop off the clothes, picture, obituary and order of service.

Thank the Lord we did not stay as long as we did before at the other places. We had to go home and call everyone to inform them of the arrangements. The visitation would be Friday night and the funeral on Saturday. This would allow for our out of town family members to be able to make the drive without jeopardizing taking time off from work. We are in a recession. People do not need to take off work unnecessarily. Because we have so many family members out of town, we wanted it on a Saturday even though we had to wait a week.

## October 29, 2009

Well, I spent the day getting myself physically ready for the funeral. Mommie and I went to Security Square Mall. I got my hair done, my manicure, my pedicure, and picked out a dress to wear to the funeral. The rest of the day was spent at home on the phone.

## October 30, 2009

Well, the viewing is today from four to eight pm at Vaughn Green Funeral Home on Baltimore National Pike. We had to be there at three pm to approve her appearance before the actual visitation. There were some minor changes that we requested physically to her facial area. Once they did that, we were very pleased. I thought that I could only stand to be there for an hour. Boy, was I mistaken. There were so many people, oh my God, how could we leave. Everyone would laugh and talk about how Grandma was. She was the same with everyone and with every organization with which she was affiliated. She was always the life of the party! She would cut up bad, no matter where she was or who she was with.

Stories were the same from everyone: her bowling league, Alzheimer's Group [she did not have it, but served as Support Group Facilitator for several years], friends from exercise class, all of the choirs with whom she sung, neighbors, family and friends.

I did not think that I would be able to handle it as well as I did, but I think that by talking with others, it helped to add on to the memories. There were so many people—people in the room, people in the hall, people outside, etc. It was great seeing so many of Grandma's friends; some that I have not seen since I was a very little girl.

For me to say that I was only going to be there for an hour, they had to run us out of there. It was past eight o'clock and people acted like they did not even want to go home. But you know if Grandma were alive, that is how it would be.

When we got home, well, the out-of-towners started rolling in. We did not know that so many had decided to stay with us. We had already had a house full with me, Charles, the boys, my sister-in-law, her hubby, my niece, and my mother-in-law. Then we had a group of cousins from Red Springs, North Carolina and Rock Hill, South Carolina. When I say groups, I mean groups, not no one, two or three people. Many of my in-laws (my father-in-law, cousins, aunts and uncles) from Charles' side of the family came until I could not believe it. I really did not expect the outpouring of love. Many of them served as pallbearers. They thought it not robbery to make the long ride up. Grissett family, . . . you truly represented. They thought the world of Grandma and vice versa. Grandma meant that much to them and even each one of them had stories to tell about Grandma. You could not help but laugh. You could not cry after all of the stories everyone told. You were too busy laughing!

## *October 31, 2009*

Well, today is the funeral at ten thirty at The Mount Moriah Baptist Church. The wake is at ten o'clock. It is something when you got a house full of twenty-five people trying to get ready for a funeral with only one full bath and two half baths. Wow! There were not many who cried as we got ready at the house. It was as if everyone was getting together to go to a party to see Grandma.

I was really proud of myself at how I carried myself. I was always known for telling people that when Grandma would die, well, you might as well dig a grave for me right beside her. It was a pun on words, of course. I guess when someone is sick, you expect death to follow. I was really worried about my boys. They were her world and everyone who knew her knew that fact. They were all she talked about. Everyone knew about the constant trips to the Carolinas to see her children. Yeah, it was always about me until I had those two boys for her.

We had prayer in the house and gathered all the vehicles together. We arrived at church and did the line-up. We processed into the church. So far. So good. There were some tears but no one falling out and trying to get in the casket. Under any other circumstances, that probably would have been me. I can see it now. Both Edie and Mommie would have slapped me. Grandma would not have had that either!

The service was awesome! Mommie, Edie and I all agreed that Grandma would have been pleased. The singing was fantastic! I could see and hear Grandma up there on the choir stand with her fellow choir members. She really loved singing!

After church services, we left and went to Arbutus Memorial Park for the "entombment". I learned new vocabulary. "Entombment" is burial above ground and "internment" is burial below ground. The entombment service was also great and was a first for many. Myself included! Well, so much for digging a grave beside her for me.

There was a brief service in a glass building. We all proceeded to the crypt site where the casket was placed in the crypt. We then watched them seal the crypt. And that was it. After the entombment services, we went back to the church for the repast.

Throughout the entire service, it seemed more like a family reunion. You know, that is the only time you see relatives—weddings and funerals. The repast was good. Some got lost in the traffic from Arbutus back to the church. But everyone eventually made it back. Everything was good. Grandma would have been cutting up. Most of the relatives left on Saturday night. For sure, everyone had to be gone by Sunday because that is when I have to head back to North Carolina.

I had to report back to Duke on Monday, November second. God worked everything out. We headed 95 South four cars deep. We drove Grandma's car back (95 Buick Century) which was going to be CJ's car. I always told my boys that they are blessed children. How is he getting another car (95 Buick Century) and already had a car (96 Nissan Altima) sitting at the house for him—and he does not even have his license??? He has always been in love with Grandma's car. I guess because it is not a manual drive. The Century is a really good car—1995 (fourteen years old) with 87,000 original miles, one owner. That car was not hurting for anything. There was a hole in the radiator which Charles fixed before we left Baltimore. There was also a hole in the muffler and we got that fixed when we got back to Lumberton. Grandma always took care of anything she had.

## *November 2, 2009*

Well, Mommie went with me to Duke this time. This was the first time she was able to go with me. We got some blood work done and another dreaded bone marrow biopsy. Yes, this makes my third bone marrow biopsy. OUCH!!! It was just like before. I also had to bring my twenty-four hour urine so they can check my kidneys out. The nurse practitioner thought she was going to do it and it would be no problem. They have always underestimated my size from day one. She stuck that huge needle in me but to no avail. She asked the tech who was with her if she wanted to try. I believe that because she saw how difficult everything was, she did not want to risk it. She then told us that she would get someone who was more experienced at these than she was.

She got a doctor and she could not do it either. I told them the difficulty everyone experienced from the other biopsies. Of course, they said the same things that the others had said, "Your bones and tissue are extremely hard". They stuck and turned that thing as if they were digging through a rock for gold. They eventually had to call another doctor (a male this time) and he, with much difficulty, did finally perform the biopsy. All four of them said when they left that this was not a typical bone marrow biopsy. Mommie visually showed me how they were doing everything since she saw it all. Of course, I am on my stomach so I cannot see anything. It's a wonder that I have bones or blood left.

I gave myself a day to heal up. Mommie and I drove back to Baltimore on Wednesday. We had to finalize things and continue cleaning up. Tomorrow (Friday, November six) is Mommie's birthday. I want to do something for her but do not know what. Everyone is always keeping me under the gun so I can't just leave and get something. Edie and I took Mommie to Applebee's for dinner. We had also planned on taking her to see Tyler Perry's new movie, *Precious*, [which opens today] only to find out later that is was showing in select areas and Baltimore was not one of them. What kind of mess is that?

## *November 5, 2009*

Hope everything is going well with everyone. Yeah, it's been a while so you know this will be a long one. Get in the recliner and get you a cup of coffee (or if you are like me, hot chocolate or hot tea will do).

Thank you for all of your condolences (prayers, cards, flowers, phone calls, etc.) It meant alot to me. I tell you what—this healing process of dealing with Grandma's passing will definitely take way much longer than my cancer process. It is so difficult to lose the matriarch of your family. The woman I grew up with at the hip all of my life. Everything went very well though. I handled myself better than I thought that I would. I was very concerned about how the boys would react, especially Michael. He does not do funerals well at all. Charles and the boys were good overall. Mommie is doing well. I think that we have all had our moments but not in front of each other. We are all trying to stay strong for the other. Grandma would be very proud.

I will be leaving back for Lumberton on Sunday. Duke called me on Tuesday and the preliminary results say that I do not have to go through another cycle of chemo. PRAISE THE LORD! They were concerned since it's been a month that I have been gone. So, I go Tuesday all day to get all of these tests run (Heart test, lung test, Echo, EKG, Chest X-ray, Skeletal Survey, etc.) I will get my full calendar for the month then. The following week, I will have to be there for three to four days straight in one of the apartments at Duke. Day one will be to get my 'Hickman' catheter—this is the port designed specifically for transplant with the prongs sticking out and I cannot get wet. (**Boy, I'm gonna be Bionic Woman when all of this is over!**) Day two, they will begin giving me a higher dose chemo (I think Cycto or the one that begins with a M, I'll let you know for sure on Tuesday). Because this will be at such a high dose, I will need to be monitored constantly. I will be hooked up to a hydration machine for three days. A home health aide will come every two to four hours and check my IV. I must stay hydrated. They will also have to keep a watch on my kidneys and liver.

Then wait another week and I will go back for the transplant so of course, there goes my Thanksgiving and Christmas holidays. Thanks again everyone and I'll update more next week. This wasn't as long as I thought. I took a picture the night before Grandma's funeral. I posted the picture on my CaringBridge website. I guess this will be my last picture with me having hair. Remember it well . . .

## *November 11, 2009*

Well, it's been a day of recovery after being picked and poked all day on yesterday. I had a Chest X-ray, EKG, Echocardiogram, Bone

Survey, Pulmonary Function Test and eight vials of blood taken. Can you believe it? Eight vials! Everything is going well though. Still hurt some in the right butt from the biopsy (Ouch!!!).

Anyway, my future plans are to go to Duke and will have to stay from next Wednesday to Saturday (November eighteenth through the twenty-first). On Wednesday morning, I am scheduled for surgery, a port removal and a Hickman catheter placement. In other words, they will remove the current port I have. They will then place in its spot what's called a Hickman port. This port has prongs sticking out of it and I cannot under any circumstances get it wet. Wow, how is that going to work? How will I take a shower? This port is used for transplant, in addition to IV connections, etc. So, after that surgery and two hour recovery, I see the doctor, and then go to check into the apartment. At six pm, a home health aide will come to begin the IV hydration hook-up. I will have a hydration bag attached to me (the size of half a suitcase literally). It will last for twenty-four hours so the health aide will come at six pm every night to change my hydration fluids. It is important for me to stay hydrated so the remains from the chemo will not stay in my bladder. They say that would be deadly.

Thursday morning, I begin Cytoxan chemo at eight am. This will be chemo that I have been taking previously but orally. This will now be by IV and will be at a higher dose. Cytoxan will kill any remaining myeloma cells left and will stimulate my stem cells in preparation for transplant. This will also be the chemo which will give me hair loss. But thanks to the guestbook entry from my Caucasian bald brother, Paul, he says being bald isn't bad. We'll see! For that Friday and Saturday, I will have the hospital visit and lab check. If everything works well, no, **when** everything goes well, I should be discharged on Saturday, the twenty-first. I will have Sunday off.

From the 23rd-29th, okay, get this. I have to give myself a shot (Neupogen) every day. Picture that! Me? They did say me or someone that I trust. Neupogen is a drug that is used to stimulate the stem cells. I will have to have blood work (lab check) locally on Monday, Wednesday and Friday. The great thing about this is I will be home for Turkey Day. Yee-pee!!! (I am not sure how up and about I will be though) That will present a challenge since I do not know if the doctor will be open on that Wednesday and Friday (the day before and the day after Thanksgiving).

I will return to Duke and stay for the next three days (Nov 30-Dec 2) when prayerfully, my white blood cell count is greater than three thousand. I will be at Duke during this time for apheresis. Apheresis is the process of gathering my blood and separating the stem cells and freezing them and placing them in a bag while warming my blood to body temperature and putting that blood back in my body. Then I will have nothing done for a week until I return to Duke on December ninth to see the doctor, have another chest x-ray, EKG, and bloodwork (labs) and check into the apartment.

On December tenth, I will begin the Melphalan chemo, another high dose chemo. December eleventh will be day one of the stem cell infusion or transplant, whatever you wish to call it. I will have to be there with supportive care for two to three weeks so I will not be home for Christmas. I should be home the week after.

So that is the schedule they have presented to me. Keep me in your prayers. When you get a chance, sign the guestbook and send me a jokey-joke or something. I need to laugh to keep from crying.

## *November 12, 2009*

I go with Charles to Urgent Care. He has to get his DOT physical (physical for truck drivers). He has not been feeling well for about the past two weeks. When he went to the doctor, she gave him some antibiotics and told him he had a bladder infection. He was constantly going to the bathroom every fifteen to twenty minutes. He could not sleep well at night because he was constantly getting up to use the bathroom. It was difficult to drive his tractor-trailer. He stayed thirsty. He also noticed how his vision was getting blurred and he was losing weight.

It was two weeks later when he went to Urgent Care and they diagnosed him as being a diabetic and that he would have to report to his doctor first thing the next morning. His blood sugar level was above five hundred. The doctor explained that he could not give him a proper reading because his number was off the chart. This was not good. When it rains, it damn it pours! Normal range is supposed to be in the one hundreds. Well, when he reported to the doctor then they confirmed the diagnosis. They put him on insulin right away. The doctor wanted to admit him to the hospital.

He explained to the doctor that we were going out of town this weekend. He stressed to her how important this weekend was [and she knew what was going on with me anyway] and that he already had money invested in this trip. Since this was the only weekend that we have before I really get into this apheresis and transplant stuff, Charles thought that it would be a great idea for us to get away. Me, Charles, the boys, my sista, Venita, and her boys and daughter, went to the beach to a nice resort hotel for the weekend. Even though the trip was initially for me, it ended up being for him. Truth be told, he needed this trip more than I did. He definitely needed the relaxation.

It was very nice and peaceful to just hear the water and watch the ocean at night. The kids had a great time! We all had a great time! Night time was beautiful. So much has been going on all at one time. I am diagnosed with cancer, my Grandma passes away, my husband is diagnosed with diabetes, what's going to happen next? How much can a person take? Yes, it feels good to be able to enjoy the peace and quiet of the calm waters. It would be nice if every day were like this. It was good to get away and focus on life and family just briefly; even though you eventually have to get back to reality. However, Charles blood sugar level did not get better. We came back on Sunday. When we walked in the door, Charles told me to call the doctor. Well, she admitted him right away this time. No questions asked and he didn't resist. He registered at the emergency room at three o'clock pm. My sista stayed at the house with the boys until it was time for her to head back to Charlotte.

We did not get into the actual emergency room until around six o'clock pm. They did not get him checked in a room until around ten thirty that night. There is such a scare with the H1N1 virus that you cannot have but one visitor per patient. The visitor must be over the age of eighteen and they have to be an immediate family member (spouse, mother, father, sister, brother). Charles made it very clear that he wanted to see his boys before he was admitted. I was trying to figure out how this was going to happen.

Even though it seems like the world is crushing down on you and life isn't getting any better, God always has a ram in the bush. Yes, I gotta tell this story. As we went from the waiting area in ER into the urgent care room in ER, they called Charles' name and another gentleman's name at the same time. We were going to room twenty-one and the gentleman and his wife were going to room twenty-two. It was actually the same room just separated by a curtain.

Charles and the other gentleman strike up several conversations. The other gentleman has been a diabetic for the past ten or twelve years and he gave some helpful advice to Charles about different things he did to regulate his blood sugar. (That's not why he was there at the hospital though) Then his wife gave us information on requesting Diabetic Education that is given by the hospital. How does she know this??? She knew this information because **she works for the hospital.** Only we did not know this at that time. We kindly accepted the information she gave us.

Charles and this guy talked and cut up for a while (You know Southeastern Regional keeps you for hours). You would have thought that we all knew each other forever. His wife provided us with so much information and connections (Ain't God good?) It came time for the boys to see Charles . . . this was difficult with the H1N1 stuff and all the limits on hospital visitation policies. Do you know that even though we waited almost two hours, she had her connections and allowed the boys [one at a time and only with her] to see Charles? As you can tell, I am not revealing any names because I do not want anyone to get in trouble and I am sure that they would not even if I did mention their name because it was when she came to get the boys that I saw she had placed her SRMC badge on and who she was . . . Wow! (The Bible says that we should watch how we treat people because you never know when you will be entertaining angels unawares!!!)

It is amazing how God places you in the right place at the right time with the right people. So, yes, now I am taking care of the caregiver. We know Charles will be in the hospital for a while. They want his blood level to get in the one hundreds before they release him. Thank goodness my mom was already coming even though she was going to be staying at home to put the boys on the bus. She will now have to be at Duke with me. We are making arrangements for someone to be at the house to put the boys on the bus. (God has already worked that out too!)

Well, I stayed Sunday, Monday and Tuesday at the hospital with Charles. I had to report to Duke on Wednesday when Charles was going to be taking me, but now Mommie was going with me. Boy, did I hate to leave him. Keep praying for me and the family. I love all of you and hope that somehow you are encouraged by taking the time to read the website, even though sometimes it seems to me like I am always bringing depressing news. But I also feel (even more deeply) that someone is being strengthened. Like I told Charles on Friday, everything happens for a reason. Well, I don't mean to cut this short but I need to eat so I can take my meds. Been busy all day as you can see. If you happen to be near or at SRMC, Charles is in room 731. I am sure that he would love to see you.

## *November 18, 2009*

I had to have surgery at eight o'clock in the morning. I am to get my old port removed and have my Hickman catheter port placed in my right chest. This port has two prongs sticking out. This port is used for apheresis and the bone marrow stem cell transplant.

I told Mommie that I have been jolly throughout this whole process until now. I am no longer jolly. Just in alot of pain. I'm weak. I'm worn down now. I have never been in a capacity to ask someone to do every little thing for me. Not that I am above that, just have never been in that situation. Reminds me about when the pastor did the eulogy at Grandma's funeral: *"Singing a familiar song in an unfamiliar place"*. I am in an unfamiliar place dealing with an unfamiliar situation. I am so used to doing for others. I felt so bad last night asking Mommie to do this, get that, put this back, comb my hair, get the suitcase, get my clothes, can I get a glass of orange juice, etc, etc. I just want to cry. I cannot take this anymore.

I can barely move my body, let alone I have to carry this machine with a pump to constantly pump the hydration fluids in me. I have to carry it everywhere. To the bathroom. To the edge of the bed. To the kitchenette area. I am just confined to the space in the apartment so where else was I going to go? I just feel so, so helpless to have to ask for literally everything. I almost wanted to ask Mommie to go to the bathroom for me and I thought "Wait a minute. I can do that by myself", except that I had to carry this suitcase with me. I can only use my left hand for anything that I must do. I can have nothing in my right hand heavier than a soda can. (I should have asked him was that an empty soda can or a full soda can?) Dressing is crazy. I can't dress myself, comb my hair—nothing! Don't think I didn't try. Boy, I am sore!!! Mommie had to tear the straps off of my shirt last night because I am hooked up to this machine. I can't just take my clothes off over my head. (UUUUGGGGG!!!!!!) We did not think about that when they hooked me up.

I just wanted to lie in the bed this morning. I asked Mommie, why the doctors couldn't come to the apartment and give me the stuff. It was a job to get up and get ready considering I can hardly move. It's raining here in Durham too!!! Sleeping weather. Ahhhh!

I am laying here now getting all of these meds through this sore catheter port and going to the bathroom every hour on the hour. The Cytoxin is very toxic and I have to constantly flush myself so the toxins do not remain in my bladder. Well, they have just given me some stuff that they said will make me fall asleep and I am feeling it.

## November 20, 2009

Well, I did not fight the sleep UNTIL the nausea kicked in and oh my God, did it kick in! They said the Cytoxin causes nausea really bad and it does. I don't know the full story. I did hear them say they had to get me off the floor. They had to get me out of the hospital in the wheelchair. All I did when I got back to the apartment was sleep.

I did not have to be at the hospital until ten o'clock this morning. Everyone was really pleased at how I looked because they said they could not recognize me yesterday. Today was an okay day. Had alot of nausea this morning as I tried to eat a bagel. I am feeling tired and restless. They had to give me some potassium and calcium today. It was low. Other than that, the rest of my blood work was good along with my urine.

I just got back in the apartment. Everything's good. I'm gonna rest. Hopefully and prayerfully, if everything is good tomorrow, I should be discharged from this hydration unit and from the hospital on Nov. 30th.

## November 22, 2009

Well, alot has transpired since my last posting on Friday. Not good at all. You know, I checked out of the apartment on Saturday and they told me oh, we have you checking out on Sunday. (No way, baby,

I'm outta here!) We go and one of the doctors checks me out and she asked me at the end, "Is 9:15 a good time?" I said for what? She replied, 'For your appointment on tomorrow'. What appointment? I had to tell her, doc, my schedule said if my labs (blood work) were good and my urine was good that I would be discharged. She looked in my report and replied, "Oh yes, you are right."

Well, my labs were okay and so was my urine. Yes, we are almost gone. Then the nursing assistant comes in to change the dressing on my port. She notices that there was some drainage at the port area and it was fresh. Okay, clean it up and let's go! Well, she had to report it to the nurse who in turn brought my doctor and the doctor on call to me. They picked and poked at the port area. Boy, was it tender! (That hurt!) But even more so, it was full of pus. This is a bad sign of infection.

So, you know who's not going to da house! They had to take blood cultures from my arm and then from the port area. It will take about twenty-four hours to get the results back from this. In the meantime, they tell me that I will have to be hooked up to antibiotics to clear the infection. They will also have to remove the port. WHAT? I just had this thing placed in me three days ago—are you kidding?

Apparently, I got up too fast from the recliner and my blood pressure dropped big time. I just remember getting up and telling the nurse I had to go to the bathroom. I never made it! I got dizzy and all I can remember is, "How did I end up on the floor again?" There was much nausea and vomiting. Mommie was on one side and the nurse was on the other. They had to sit me in the wheelchair to place me in the room with a bed.

Now, I had to have the port removed. OOOOGGGGHHHHHH!!!! It's amazing how long and tedious the process is for the surgery to have this port placed in you and how quickly the doctor was able to remove it. I mean she just pulled the port out like she was pulling out a string. Man, I am wondering if she pulled out some other organs when she pulled out that port. That port is connected in my arteries and near my heart. I wanna make sure that I leave with all the same organs that I came in with. Then I have to have three hours worth of antibiotics pumped into me. Man, now we are back to the arm deal! My arms really enjoyed not being poked for a while.

Well, you know by this time, since I was not coming home and I was having all of these issues, Charles grabbed the boys and headed

95 North. After the antibiotics, I was to report back to Duke in the morning. They came and spent the night with us in the apartment that I was trying so hard to check out off (and ended up staying). Charles moved so fast. They did not pack any clothes or anything. I know. I know. He was worried about me. I felt so bad for my Mommie because it took her so long to pack everything in the suitcases and then in the car and now she had to unpack again. And I could not help. Well, at least the boys were there to help. What was a comfortable room for two people ended up feeling a little tight for five people. (Hey, who was taking care of Snoop?) So Sunday, I reported back to the hospital for three hours of antibiotics again.

They told me I had to have three more days of antibiotics. Are you kidding me? (You guys said I would be home this week) Well, they told me I could come home over night, but I had to report back to Duke Monday morning at ten thirty am and resume the antibiotics and be there for three days.

Man, it was a "ruff" weekend. It was good to be home for a few hours—that's all it was. No sooner than I got home, got a little bit of rest, I had to get up to go back to Duke.

## *November 23, 2009*

Well, it is Monday. Mommie and I had everything all packed up AGAIN and ready to stay for three days. Got my labs done (good) and my antibiotics (three hours again) and had a "rectal something" where they stuck a swab up my butt to see if I have VRE. Everyone has this done to check to see if you have a bacteria/virus called VRE.

"VRE stands for Vancomycin-resistant enterococci which are a type of bacteria called enterococci that have developed resistance to many antibotics, especially vancomycin. Enterococci bacteria live in our intestines and on our skin, usually without causing problems. Experts do not know exactly why some people become infected with VRE and others do not. But they do know that VRE infections are more likely to develop when antibotics such as vancomycin are used often. Given enough time, bacteria can change so that these antibotics no longer work well.[2]

I asked what would happen if someone has this? Do they give you antibiotics for this too? She told me that if someone has it from this point on, they are placed in confinement each time they come to the hospital. (We will see how that goes)

Two of my doctors went back and forth and said they thought the three days of antibiotics was enough already. So far, the culture was looking negative, but my doctor (who happened to be there on Saturday when everything happened) said I needed to have more antibiotics. After back and forth, back and forth, my nurse practitioner told me that I could have the antibiotics done locally at the Gibson Cancer Center. Anything beats driving that distance and being away from home.

My original schedule stated that I start my neupogen shot today from now until Sunday. Well, we eventually get home about six tonight to find out that I have to take two shots instead of one. It was because of the amount that each needle contained. I already do not like needles. Why couldn't they put the whole six hundred mcg in one needle??? The needles are three hundred mcgs. OOGGHH!! I figure I'll take it at night and I could go to bed and sleep it off. Mommie and Charles are debating about who is going to give me the shot. I knew I was not! I told them since it is two shots, Mommie can give me one and Charles can give me the other. That will solve that!

It ended up that Mommie gave me the shots and I would squeeze Charles' hand. Boy, did he complain that I squeezed his hand too hard. You would squeeze hard too if that shot was being pushed in your stomach! (Big baby!) I thank God for my mother. She really did not want to give me the shot after having to give Grandma a shot three times a day for how long . . . All I know is that I could not give it to myself. Not with my paranoia of blood and needles. It wasn't gonna happen.

I reported to the Gibson Cancer Center on Tuesday at one o'clock in the afternoon. When I went on Tuesday, they asked me if I wanted to come on Wednesday at eight thirty am because being hooked up to the antibiotics is a three to four hour process. Because Thursday is Thanksgiving, I have to go the hospital on Thursday or Friday.

Well, it is a relatively boring process to just sit there and be hooked up to the IV for three hours. At least I did get to watch television. And they fed me on Wednesday. Also, on Wednesday and Friday, I am suppose to have lab work done so they can see where my counts are.

# *November 25, 2009*

Well, here is my latest update. It's amazing how things change in the course of a night. Since my last update, let's see Duke has called and said that I need seven days of antibiotics. So, that meant to go to the Cancer Center here locally (which I did tell you on the last update but I thought it was just that one day—Tuesday). So, I went Tuesday and today. Now, Monday, Wednesday and Friday, I am suppose to have lab work done just so they can keep abreast of my counts and everything. So, today my blood work indicated that my hemoglobin was extremely low. 7.5 or something. So, they are saying that I should be extremely tired and weak—like too weak to pick up my hand or walk even. I, on the other hand, felt fine. God is good! I walked right outta there!

I do know how it feels when it is at the point of not being able to do anything. But, to their surprise, I did not feel like that. They told me that I needed a blood transfusion. Say what? Man, no! I refused and they discharged me. Of course, when they faxed the report to my doctor at Duke, well, she called me on my cell phone as we were driving back home on I-95. She said that my count was very low and a transfusion was not optional. It was required. I need to go to the hospital on tomorrow and Friday for antibiotics. However, now, when I go on Friday, I will basically be there all day because I will have the three hours for antibiotics and several hours for the transfusion. This is needed because when I go to Duke on Monday for the surgery and apheresis, I cannot be weak, like I am now—even though I do not feel it.

So, that's that! For those just tuning in on joining this journey with me, it's all good. Like I have said from the very beginning, this journey is not all for me, but for others. I cannot put into words everything that God has done since June 17, 2009. I talked with a nurse at the Gibson Cancer Center (a nurse whom I have never met) and she was just so amazed at my story. She was in awe at how I looked and how I talked calmly about my situation and what I had gone through. She asked me so many questions regarding my case and this and that. She just sat there like she could not believe me. She said "You are so lucky!". I told her that luck had nothing to do with it. "I am blessed!"

I had to pre-register today for my appointments at the hospital on tomorrow and Friday. Initially I had a problem with one lady who needed more information that I did not have so I had to call the Cancer Center and get some additional information. You know sometimes we get frustrated when someone gets in our way as we are traveling somewhere in a hurry, but it could be a blessing in disguise. Maybe this is God's way of having you avoid being in a traffic accident. That was how I felt about this conversation. I got so irritated because I thought the pre-registration process should have been smoother. Well, when I called back to the hospital to complete the pre-registration, I spoke to a woman named Teresa. The Lord meant for us to talk. She was my blessing in disguise. That is why there was an issue with the first woman. It was so I could call back and talk to Teresa. We had a wonderful time talking about the Lord and how awesome He is. I was telling her my story and we just had a great time on the telephone and my pre-registration was a seamless process.

Sometimes it may seem like things are just going wrong, but God is always working through it all. I keep telling y'all that I do not like to keep sending what seems like bad news, but it's really all good!!! God is still working and He is just awesome.

Like I told Ms. Teresa, you just can't put it into words . . .

The awesomeness of God . . . . PRICELESS!!!!!!

I hope everyone enjoys their Thanksgiving holiday and enjoy your family and friends. Be truly thankful!

## *November 26, 2009*

My mother and I reported at nine o'clock on Thanksgiving Day to Five South at Southeastern Regional Medical Center to have my antibiotics. We wondered about everything when we got off the elevator. We made a right turn and walked and walked. The floor was completely empty. I mean we circled the entire floor, room to room, and even the nurse's station. We walked back to the elevators. We realized that had we made a left turn when we got off the elevator, we would have seen the sign on the door which read "Press the Grey Button". We did and they were expecting us. (Reading is fundamental.) We had gone to Five North, an empty section of the hospital.

The nurse tried to hook me up and asked me how come I did not have an IV in me already. I explained how I have been picked and poked each day all week. I had to alternate arms each day. The nurse told me that they should have stuck an IV in me and it could stay for three or four days. I did not know to ask for or suggest that. That would have been great. They had a hard time trying to find a vein. They did not want to use the veins in my arm, but those are always the ones that stand out. I have never had issues before with finding veins.

They prefer to use the hand or wrist. Well, it took two nurses and thirty minutes and two pokes only to realize that they did not get a vein. They tried in my right back hand and my left wrist. The left wrist hurt worse than giving birth. Oh my God, the pain!!! They tried to call the IV team who never responded—it must have been because it was Thanksgiving Day. They said they never like to stick an IV in the arm except as a last minute resort. Hello? Looks like this is a last resort.

They asked me if I wanted to keep the IV in my arm and we would not have to go through this tomorrow. I agreed. What could I lose? My arm already looks like I am a crackhead. The downfall would be that I would have to keep my arm extended for a whole day. At least it is my left arm. I can still go home and eat Thanksgiving dinner, with my right hand, with my family.

Since I have to get a blood transfusion and my antibiotics tomorrow, the nurse asked me if I wanted to come about six-thirty in the morning. It would be three to four hours for the antibiotics and another three to four hours for the blood transfusion so I agreed. The earlier I get in, the earlier I would get out.

After my antibiotics, Mommie and I went home where everyone was waiting on us to eat. Things were quite different. Charles told me to look at things in that I could have been at Duke during this week as originally planned. I guess he was right. I am thankful to be home with my family and friends. You know they say, it is two ways to look at a glass—half empty or half full. I'd rather look at it being half full.

## November 29, 2009

I had my antibiotics on Thursday. Got home at two pm with everyone waiting for me to come home so we can eat. It was good to be with family. It was a blessing to be able to have food to eat, a place to eat, friends to be with. It sounds so simple but there are really people who are not able to say that on Thanksgiving Day, or any other day, for that matter.

Got disturbing news Thursday night that I had a cousin in DC who passed away Thanksgiving morning. I was so upset. I mean, I just spent time with this cousin at Grandma's funeral. She was not sick or anything. She just didn't wake up. Some hours later got another call that an uncle in NY passed away also on Thanksgiving Day. (Boy when it rains, it pours!) I feel really bad because I know that I will not be able to attend either funeral because I am about to start this transplant phase and neither family member knows about my situation. We really did not inform many people on Grandma's side of the family because we did not want it to get back to her.

On Thursday, the nurses asked me if I would come at six am because since I was suppose to be there all day, the earlier I got there the better. I said why not. And I was literally there ALL day. I was there from six-thirty Friday morning and was discharged at twelve thirty am (30 minutes after midnight) on Saturday. Then I had to go home to get those two Neupogen shots. Had been running a slight fever. Getting ready to pack and prepare for the next three days at Duke. Pray for me!

### Remember, no matter what state you are in, be content!!!

I report to the hospital at six thirty the next morning. They did not start right away. My antibiotic had to get ordered. So that takes time and then there is paperwork. I had to also have my labwork done. They did not start until around nine or so. Okay, so I was here for three hours and we have done what? Nothing. Yeah, that's what I said. Three hours! Then it was paperwork for my transfusion. I also had to get typed for my blood—meaning they go through a process with Red Cross to get my same blood type and I also had to get only filtered irradiated blood.

Irradiated blood is given to prevent rare complications of transfusion called transfusion-associated graft-versus-host disease (TA-GvHD). TA-GvHD is a rare but serious complication of blood transfusion caused by white blood cells (lymphocytes) in the blood transfused. Even a very small number of lymphocytes may recognize the patient receiving the blood as "foreign" and cause a severe illness or even death.[3]

I needed two grams of blood. One gram would last for four hours. So, I had the one gram of blood first. A few minutes had passed and I could hear the nurse on the phone mentioning my name. Well, praise be to God, he was looking at the paperwork and realized that I had blood, which had white blood cells. Of course, I am not suppose to have this type of blood because my white blood count is low and have to stay low. He came and went through the process of unhooking me. I asked him how this would affect me considering blood already began flowing through my body.

He mentioned that in those twenty minutes or so, I only received a few cc's. Not enough to do any major damage to me. I dread to imagine what would have happened had he not read the orders and knew what to look for. So now, we have to wait for my correct blood. We finally got that going. That was three hours or so. And then the next gram. In between each of these, they did feed me breakfast, lunch and dinner. Can you believe that I did not leave the hospital until twelve thirty Saturday morning? That was a whole eighteen hours. It was as if I was at work and did some overtime. OMG! I am so glad that it was now over. This ends my seven days of antibiotics. Seven! The number of completion. Yes!

I report back to Duke on November thirtith, which was my original date for apheresis anyway. I must report to the Bone Marrow Department first at eight in the morning for labwork. I will then be shuttled to Radiology for my surgery. Yes, we will try this again. They will place another Hickman port in me. Hopefully, we will get no infection this time. Then I will report back to Bone Marrow for the results to see if I am able to proceed with apheresis.

Just to let you know what apheresis is. Recent studies suggest that it may be possible to shorten the length of time your blood counts will be low after transplant by using the blood stem cells collected by leukapheresis (Apheresis). These stem cells will help blood counts recover after high dose chemotherapy.

Stem cell leukapheresis is a standard outpatient procedure that takes approximately four to six hours. Blood is withdrawn from a central line catheter (Hickman), or from IV's placed in arm veins, and processed through a blood cell separator. The part of the white blood cell layer that contains the stem cells is collected and the rest of the blood is returned to the body in a continuous process. A small amount of plasma is also collected for the lab to process the stem cells.

To prevent blood from clotting in the machine, an anticoagulant (or blood thinner) is mixed with the blood as it is withdrawn and circulates through the machine. This anticoagulant is short acting and will be effective only as the blood circulates through the machine. It may cause some numbness or tingling in lips, fingers, and/or feet. Possible side effects, which are rare, may include fever, chills, infection, and anemia (resulting from red cell breakage as it circulates through the machine). While very rare, blood loss may occur. This may be due to a breakage of the tubing or containers used to collect your cells. Machine failure may also occur.

They told me once I arrived to prepare to be there until Friday, and not Wednesday, like originally expected. They could not begin the apheresis today. They did begin apheresis on Tuesday, December first. I am hooked up to a machine which collects the blood and separates the stem cells and plasma and returns the blood back to me during the stem cell transfusion.

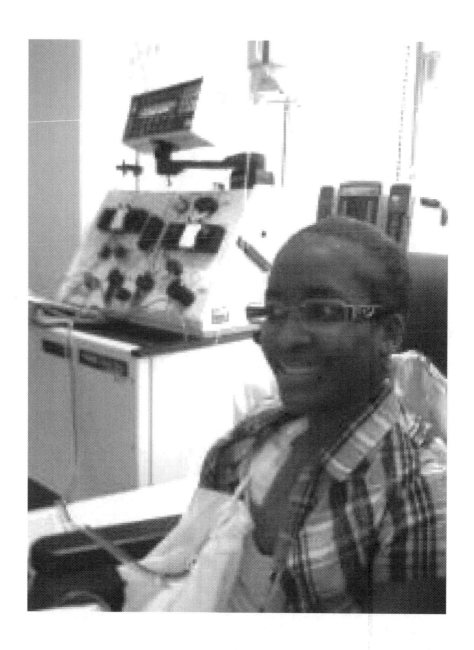

## December 1, 2009

If I have learned nothing else during this transition, I have learned that I need to pack for double the days they tell me. I was suppose to be here until Wednesday. NOT! They wait to tell me when I get up here to be prepared to stay until Friday. WHAT! I have been here since Monday and have been sent home everyday. I have learned that my WBC (white blood cell) count has to be at least three before they can even look at my stem cell count.

Well, my WBC was .9 on yesterday. Yes, point nine. (Can I get a whole number?) So, we were sent home on yesterday. Today, my WBC was 4.8 which allowed them to be able to check out my stem cell count. My stem cell count was 4.9. It must be at least ten for them to begin the apheresis.

So we are half way there. Maybe we can begin something tomorrow. They are still giving me the neupogen shots (shots to stimulate the stem cells). On my calendar they gave me, I thought I only had seven days of that and it was over. NOT again! They are still giving it to me. Not my Mommie. I know she is relieved.

Don't have much to say since nothing is going on. Oh, guess what, I must have ate alot during Thanksgiving. I weighed in at 130 on yesterday and 131 today. I had been 127-128.

To those who know how I eat, I would have made you proud. Trust and believe, my eating has not been disturbed during this process at all. Hope everyone enjoyed their holidays and time off. Looking forward to being able to give you some relevant news on tomorrow.

## December 2, 2009

I'm hooked up!!! Don't know what my count was today. Don't care. I only care that it is high enough for them to hook me up and begin my stem cell collection. Yee-Pee!!! I was too excited to hear what the count was. I gotta be hooked up for six hours. Ooohhhhh!!! You have to take the good with the bad. I asked Mommie to take a picture so I can show everyone. We are doing well. I'm surprised my hair has not come out yet like they said. I have it in a ponytail. It is shedding like crazy though. I am so scared of it coming out that I have not done anything to it and I won't do anything to it until I definitely have to. I figure if I don't do anything to it, it will be fine. Oh, I'm back to 130 lbs. Thought that after eating all of that pizza and drinking sunkist sodas last night, I would surely have made the 135 mark. I was just so excited. Wanted to share my news! Guess I will not leave here until five pm.

## *December 5, 2009*

Today is the Marietta Christmas Parade. It has been raining since last night. Not sure if they are going to have the parade or not. Charles and Michael got up at six thirty am to go the barber shop to get their hair cut. Charles did not really need a hair cut. He still got a bald head and Michael got a fade. Charles and his club members are riding their motorcycles in the parade. My mother took Michael to the parade. Michael wanted to ride the motorcycle with Charles but due to the cold weather, we did not want him to get sick.

Since I was home by myself and my mother had been complaining and wondering when I was going to wash my hair, I decided that I would go ahead and wash my hair. It had been straight the entire time since I had been keeping it in a ponytail. I cannot remember the last time that I washed it. After I washed and conditioned my hair, I felt that it was clumpy. I was about to dry it and I figured that I should try to comb through it to straighten it out again. I tried and tried and tried until I was physically tired. But to no avail. That does not take much for me now to get tired easily.

I gave up and just cried to myself. I could not stop crying. I knew that this was the moment. They told me two weeks after the Cytoxan that I would lose my hair and today was exactly two weeks to the day. Once Charles came home and saw what happened, he called his friend, Bunny. Mr. Bunny, a gentleman who has been cutting my husband's hair since he was a young boy. He and his wife came to the house. Bunny cut and shaved my hair. WOW! All I can say is "Thanks Bunny!" I have to represent and still look like the DIVA that I am.

When Charles came home, I told him that I was going to look like him. He smiled. He said that is why he had his head cut bald like he did earlier this morning—for me! He did not want me to feel out of place or uncomfortable. He remembered what Duke said about my hair coming out. Guess he took heed to what they were saying more than I did.

## *December 7, 2009*

I had to pick up some last minute prescriptions before I leave on Wednesday. I had to take Michael to his dentist appointment finally. I had to cancel the last two previous appointments because they required that a parent bring the child. With my scheduling back and forth at Duke, I nor Charles had been able to go. This appointment was crucial because the cleaning had been put off long enough. I also needed to ask them about Michael grinding his teeth at night. They stated because he is in this stage of still losing his baby teeth and getting his permanent teeth, this is just a phase that he is going through. They stressed that he will grow out of it. Okay, we'll see.

## *December 8, 2009*

Today my husband's uncle, Pitt, passed away. (The rain is still pouring. When will it stop?!) He had been in the Hospice House for a while. We still have wonderful memories of how funny Pitt was. We spent some of the evening with Aunt Pearl and other family members at her home. I felt so bad because I knew that I was leaving on tomorrow for Duke and Charles and I would miss the funeral. We are going to miss you, Pitt!

## *December 9, 2009*

Well, today is the day. I had to report to Duke at one thirty pm. I first reported to Adult Bone Marrow Transplant. After getting my labs, I was shuttled to Radiology for my Chest X-ray and EKG. We then talked with the doctor to discuss what to expect for the next few weeks that I will be here. After that, we checked into the apartment.

Duke has placed us in a nice two-bedroom, two bathroom, fully-furnished apartment home which will be my residence from today until December 29, 2009. We checked in and got settled. Charles went to get some food and a few household items. It is as if we are at home away from home. This will truly be a different Christmas. One that none of us will ever forget. I am thankful that at least we are able to be together.

## December 10, 2009

Today, I have my high dose Melphalan chemo. This is in preparation for my stem cell infusion (Bone Marrow Stem Cell Transplant) on tomorrow. Melphalan has the job of killing off any remaining myeloma cells.

## December 11, 2009

Today is what they have been calling my birthday. I will have my stem cell bone marrow transplant today. Before they told me that I gave them 8.5 million stem cells. The final confirmed count was 9.8 million stem cells. WOW! That was great to hear. I always like being the overachiever!!! I thought that I would be hooked up to the machine again since that was the way they took the blood out. I thought they would go about the same process, but it was quite different.

They gave me my blood back through a very huge syringe. Unfortunately, Charles did not get to see the 'apheresis' process. Just as you get hooked up to an IV, they hook up this syringe to you and inject this huge tube of stuff in you. They told us that I would stink after the process was over. They said Charles would notice but I would not because it was my blood and I would be immune to it. When we left, Charles kept looking at me and saying, "You do stink. You don't smell it?" I could not smell anything.

Now, the process is that my white blood cell count is going to go down and basically bottom out to zero and then it will gradually go up. I will have to report to Duke EVERYDAY, yes, that includes Saturdays and Sundays. I will have to pay my seventy copay everyday. That is four hundred ninety dollars a week. It is expensive being sick. I do not care if you got insurance or not. If I am paying four hundred ninety dollars a week with insurance, I wonder what I would have to pay if I did not have insurance. It was different paying seventy dollars when the visits were twice a week. That was just one hundred forty dollars a week. Staying healthy sure is costly. Just imagine if I did not have insurance. They will check my bloodwork and vital signs. It's very important that I do not experience any signs of fever. During this process, one or more of the electrolytes (Potassium, Magnesium, Calcium) are knocked out of whack. After checking my labs, they will provide me with whatever electrolytes or supplements that I need.

This has been a treacherous road these past few days. None like I have experienced before. I'm not having a taste for foods (Oh God that is not me!!!) I'm very weak and that is killing me! But they said that this would be part of the process. My counts are going to bottom out and then go back up.

Things could be so much the other way. There is a lady here and Charles was talking with her husband. She could not even get the transplant because of her physical conditions. He reminded me how blessed I am that I am able to physically go through this 'cause it is a battle. I have always been marked as "Superwoman" but I think "Superwoman" has met her match now. I do not know if I can continue on with this. This is so overwhelming.

For those who have asked, I am not in a room at Duke, per se. I am at Duke all day, usually from 8-3 pm. My address while I am here is:

Independence Park Apartments
Apartment 703
215 William Penn Plaza
Durham, NC 27704

One of my cousins brought my boys up here tonight to visit us for the weekend. When Charles had learned of this news, he decided to go the pawn shop and buy a television. The apartment only provided one television in the living room. He went and bought two televisions for $96. We won't hear any fuss now. CJ can watch the game on one television. Michael can watch Nickelodeon on the other television. Charles and I can watch television in the living room.

Well, we had fun the weekend. The boys adjusted very well. I know that they were not used to seeing their mother in the condition that she was in. I am having difficulty getting up and moving around. Everything is just becoming so hard for me. I am throwing up like crazy too. We keep a trashcan on the right side of my recliner.

Charles ended up having to take the boys back home on Sunday. His uncle was going to meet him half way but never answered his phone when the time arrived.

My Mommie was home that following week to take care of the boys. Friday is their last day of school for the Christmas holidays. They will all come to Durham after they get out of school and stay with me for the duration of my visit. I'll be honest and say that I am not keen on getting a Christmas tree. Not that I was not in the Christmas spirit, but I guess my mind had been on other things. Charles insisted that we get a tree. If not for us, for the boys. He was right. We needed to try to make it feel as much like Christmas as possible. He got a little tree from Family Dollar. It was kinda cute. A gold, pre-lit tree. We laughed when we noticed that some of the gifts were bigger than the tree. We purchased a gold ribbon which my nurse practitioner's mother personally hand-made. We placed that on top of the tree. That did give it a little more height. It still only came to my waist.

When Mommie and the boys came, it almost started to feel like Christmas. I know that I was still dealing with the worst part of my cancer. In everything, I always try to be positive and optimistic. It has been hard sometimes. I want to cry most of the time, and I do cry, but not in front of the boys, or anyone for that matter. I am most comfortable when everyone else around me is comfortable.

It was a trial to have to get up every day to go to Duke. The hardest part is getting up. It takes me at least ninety minutes (literally) to get ready. I do not even have to do my hair (because I have none) and it still takes me this long. My body is just so weak and tired. I want to just lie in bed forever. For the most part, my visits have been good. I always have to get at least three hours of potassium.

I had to get a blood transfusion one day. My only problem has been having fevers off and on. I would feel completely fine though. I guess I would look flush in the face. Charles or my mother would feel my face and would say that I am burning up. Then when I feel like I am burning up, they would feel me and I would physically feel fine. I could not understand it.

## December 18, 2009

It is now snowing. Charles went to Lumberton as my mother and the boys are on their way here to Durham. It was the last day of school for the holidays. Charles needed a break. He has been a trooper putting up with me. He must really love me. He could have bailed out at any time, but he didn't. I know it has been hard for him. It has been one million times worse for me. He went back to Lumberton because his motorcycle club was having a Christmas social at Golden Corral. On his way back next Thursday, he will bring my mother-in-law and her foster son for Christmas.

My sister-in-law, brother-in-law and my precious niece, Kylan, came on Christmas. We were truly blessed to have such a spacious place. We had room for everyone. Christmas isn't all about the gifts (well, let's be real, it is if you are a kid), it's about family and friends celebrating the birth of Jesus. The kids were excited to see the little bit of snow Durham had. I say little because being from Baltimore, I have seen my share of snow in my life. I know my boys get tired of me telling the same story over and over again about how I had to go to school with snow up to my knees. I did for real. I assume that they think I am telling a fictional story but it is true. My mother has to always verify the story.

## December 22, 2009

I'm getting slower and slower with this. Since my transplant on December eleventh, my count has bottomed out to zero (really below zero—less than .01). During this time, expectations are extreme fatigue (like I have never imagined), extreme low immunity system (which is why I am advised to not go out at all), diarrhea, vomiting, lack of appetite and still no taste in my mouth. They said I will not regain taste in my mouth again until thirty to thirty-five days after my counts have reached its potential.

It has really been difficult wanting to eat something (and you know I can eat) and when you get it you can't eat it because it does not taste right or you are vomiting it back up. I also have this thing where I smell something and it messes up my stomach—like I felt when I was pregnant. Yuk!

I basically sit and wait for the count to rise which usually takes on average about five days. That's about five days of torture. I go to Duke every day to have my bloodwork done. They check my vitals every day, especially my electrolytes (magnesium, calcium, phosphorus, potassium, stuff like that). Every day I have been okay except in the area of potassium. I have been getting three hours of potassium everyday because my level has been extremely low. Yesterday, it was at its lowest point (2.9), for some unknown reason, so I had to have four to five hours of potassium. (And I had a banana that morning! What in the world?$@$(&@_%^#_^ . . .)

I have been getting my neupogen shots AGAIN daily. Yes, those same shots that I had to get during Thanksgiving. Now, Mommie and Charles do not have to worry about giving me the shots. The nurses give it to me at Duke but I still have to hold someone's hand. Neupogen is what makes the cells multiply and grow. (Gimme! Gimme! Gimme!)

The past week has been miserable. I won't lie to anyone. And every person (caregiver) would come to me and say how good I look and how good I was moving. Was nobody but Jesus! 'Cause I told them that I only wish I felt the way I looked. I feel so lifeless.

Different caregivers were stating problems encountered by their patients and how I just seem to be moving along. They did not see how it is a struggle to get up and get ready and when I return from Duke, all I do is sit in the recliner until it is time to go to bed. Can't do anything else. My count yesterday did get to point two. And today it is one. They said I could leave to go home as early as next Monday but of course that is not in black and white. It all depends on my white blood count level. I was not scheduled to leave until next Tuesday anyway.

So, you all keep praying for me and keep sending me good cheer! I hope all of you have a great holiday season. Enjoy your holidays! Be very careful if you are traveling the road. They got a foot and a half of snow at home (Baltimore).

And in your prayers, please remember my paternal grandfather, Dr. William Alexander. He's in the hospital at home. He and my grandmother shared similar medical issues. He refused to take his meds over a week ago and hasn't been eating right for a while. He has been disoriented at times. So, if you remember, just say a prayer for him.

We all need to pray for each other. We need to help each other. You never know when you are going to be on the receiving end, so it is good to always be on the giving end as much as possible. Cherish your family and friends and the time spent with them. Do not worry about trivial things. It does not matter.

I got out for the first time other than to go to Duke. We went to the Wal-Mart and went to the mall. Everyone was doing some last minute shopping. I was just walking around, when I could. I got to my little niece try to play with the big kids in the little play area. It did my heart good to try and watch her go. Her five month self.

## December 25, 2009

Well, Christmas is not the same without Grandma. In previous years, if Grandma was not with us (that was rare), she was the first voice we talked to. She would call early in the morning. We would have received Christmas cards ahead of time. It is already different being here and being in this unfamiliar and unique, for lack of a better word, situation. Still very weak. I am mustering a little energy just to be able to hug my little niece. My boys loved Christmas because of the Wii game. All three of them (CJ, Michael and Charles) loved it, along with the foster-son. I am thankful to be alive and to be able to see this day. Oh, how I wish Grandma was here!!! Spent a lot of time on the phone. Everyone is sending texts with holiday wishes. We opened gifts. We ate a wonderful meal. We enjoyed the company and love of one another. I enjoyed watching my little niece trying to open her gifts.

## December 27, 2009

We are all packing up. I am supposed to be discharged tomorrow if all goes well. It is amazing how, when you travel, your luggage somehow doubles, even triples, upon returning. I guess that is because it is Christmas. Okay, I will let that one go by.

Initially, Charles said that he would pack everything in the cars Sunday night. I did have a very high fever (103.3) on Sunday night. I guess that was what made him change his mind. He said that we would just wait until after we came back from the doctor before we packed the vehicles.

I had to report back today with the intentions of leaving. We were so sure. They pulled my Hickman port out on Thursday. So they said when I came on Monday that if everything looked good, that I could go home. I mean, we all packed everything up Sunday night and you know when you travel, you go back home with more than what you left with. We were ready!

## *December 28, 2009*

Well, I went to Duke and, of course, they saw where I called in yesterday and I had the high fever. I have been having some pretty high fevers off and on for a while. When I say high, I'm talking 103.3, 102.7. I had just had a fever on Thursday and they took blood cultures. It usually takes 24–48 hours to get the results back from them. So, when I went in on Monday, they said that the cultures were negative. Thank you Jesus! They did not feel comfortable discharging me without trying to find out why I am having such high fevers off and on.

I had another fever Sunday night (103.3). When I spoke to my doctor that night, she suggested that someone get me another thermometer. I told her that I have had my thermometer for a while. Charles bought another one and we still got the same results. She told me to take some Tylenol and she would see me in the morning. My body must know when I am at Duke because every time I have a fever and then I go to Duke, I do not have a fever. I got there this morning (after taking my temp this morning—102.7) and my temp was 98.6. Go figure!

They did not want me to go home and something worse happens and I would have to drive two hours back. I could honor and respect their decision. I did not like it, but I could respect it. They said they know it is not infectious because my blood cultures came back negative. So, there are no infections in my blood system. So, they are looking at it as being something inflammatory. I forgot the medical terminology but there is a possibility that I have inflammation of the

101

lungs. If I do have this and it is not treated, it can turn very deadly. It would have to be treated with steroids. On the up side, all of my blood work is perfect!! (his exact words).

I felt bad because my mother-in-law had to go to work Monday night, so she definitely had to go back to Lumberton. Well, we packed up my car with things that we assumed we would not need for the next few days. So, she and her foster son left in my car. I just wished we could have all been leaving. I had to stay. What looks like a downfall could be a blessing in disguise.

They sent me to Radiology for a chest x-ray and to Pulmonary for a pulmonary, or breathing, test. They said that my chest x-ray was okay. My pulmonary test showed a decline in my breathing compared to my results prior to transplant.

I did not have to go to Duke on Tuesday. They told me to report back on Wednesday and most likely I would be discharged then. I needed to call them on Tuesday if I continued to have a fever. I had to monitor my temperature all day. I did it in two to four hour intervals. No fever.

One of my co-workers called me on Saturday and said that if I was not home on Monday that she was going to come and see me. I insisted that she not come. I told her that I was sure that I would be home soon and there was no need for the drive. She could see me when I get home. She called Monday and, of course, I was still there. Well, Mia **snuck** up on me and brought the whole crew (Shelia, Ms. Terry and Krysten). They know that I am very sensitive. I wanted to cry. I really enjoyed their company and their gifts. That's my "Indian" family. (You didn't know I had Indian in my blood?)

I am so glad that Mia wasn't driving. She wore that Wii game out—boxing. She and Michael just could not get enough. They had so much fun. The rest of us had fun just watching them. We also did some bowling and golf too. On top of that surprise, my best friend, Jay, for the past twenty-nine years from Baltimore also came to visit me. Life could not get any better. We talk often but his job [Senior Executive in Charge of United Way of the Tri-State (NY, NJ and CT)] keeps him very busy. I have not seen Jay since his mother passed away in August 2008. I really wanted to cry now. He brought birthday cards, Christmas cards and gifts for me for the past two years. I'm nothing but a big ball of water. We all had so much fun! I am too happy! Words cannot express . . .

## *December 30, 2009*

When I went to Duke today, they stated that they would let me go home, but, of course, to call if I showed any symptoms of fever or infection of any kind. You are talking about some happy people. Charles and the boys had already packed the jeep up this morning around six-thirty. He said he felt that we were going to leave. So, we packed up and dropped the apartment key off at the rental office so when we leave Duke, we can go straight home.

Today is December 30th—Grandma's birthday. She would have been seventy-seven years young today. I guess this was her birthday gift to me. She talked to the Commander-In-Chief [God] and said to allow her baby to go home. **HAPPY BIRTHDAY GRANDMA!**

They had us in a beautiful place. Gorgeous. But three weeks is long enough. I was about to be like Dorothy and click my heels and say "There's no place like home, there's no place like home . . ." On the one hand, I was so excited, but then on the other hand, I am going to miss the other patients that I was used to seeing every day. They were family away from home. We all encouraged each other throughout this process.

If someone was not in for that particular day, we were concerned. That is how everyone is about everyone else. We grew to be a family. I guess you could not help it when you see the same people every day. You experience the same obstacles. You encourage each other. Spouses and caregivers encourage each other. It is much easier for someone to listen or be able to understand you when you have experienced the exact same thing.

That's just like nobody can talk to me about how it feels to have a miscarriage; to have two in a consecutive row, for that matter. Sure, you can say I *can imagine* what you are going through, but you certainty cannot say that you know exactly what I am going through unless you have experienced it for yourself.

I, on the other hand, can talk to someone about the pain and emptiness you can feel inside. I can talk to someone about how I had pictures of a baby inside of me and then to go to the doctor's office and not hear a pulse during the ultrasound. And then the doctor tells you that there is no baby inside of you. You try to understand how you are looking at pictures just weeks before, of this baby inside of you, and then it is not there. And the doctors cannot explain to you what happened.

Then, in the other situation, how there is a baby growing inside of you and the baby is still there, but not breathing. You must have a D&C (Dilation and curettage). The goal of a D&C is to scrape the inside of the uterus and cervical canal to provide a sample tissue for microscopic examination. The procedure is named "dilation and curettage" because gynecologists first "dilate", or "stretch" the uterus to make it wider. Curettage involves using curette instruments to remove a sample of the endometrium to be examined later.

D&Cs are one of the most common of all gynecological operations and are performed in either hospitals or outpatient clinical settings. The most frequent reason a doctor will order a D&C is to assess the cause of abnormal or heavy vaginal bleeding. D&Cs are also used to remove tissues from the uterus after a failed pregnancy or miscarriage.[4]

I said all of that to say that caregivers of cancer patients share the same experiences and can talk to each other. It eases your mind and heart to know that you are not the only person experiencing this situation. There are many others—some better and some worse, but all similar in the steps that you take as far as medicines, medical procedures, etc.

## *January 2, 2010*

Praise God that you are able to read this. This means that God found favor on you to let you see another year. I know that God found favor on me to let me be able to come home on Wednesday. Thank you for your prayers!!!

I go back for my follow-up visit with the doctor in four weeks. Starting Tuesday, I go to my doctor at the Gibson Cancer Center every week to have my blood drawn and my lab work faxed to Duke so they can keep up with my counts. If something does not look right, then they will call me right away.

So, now I am in the beginning of this sixth month recovery period which means that I must avoid crowds at all costs. I have a "baby" immune system so for the next six months; I am still easily able to catch any type of cold, infection, etc. I can do light activity alternating with resting periods in between. They have me on a regular diet versus a neutropenic diet.

If you are neutropenic, you are experiencing a low count of white blood cells called neutrophils, which can make you susceptible to infection. Engaging in a netropenic diet lowers the risk of foodborne infections and reduces exposure to high bacteria foods. So, we thank God we are not on that anymore.

Thank you for your love, your prayers, your support, your visits and your presents!!! It's by no means over yet! I know that we are over the worse of everything! Hope everyone has a great beginning to a wonderful New Year! I'm not into the New Years resolutions stuff, but I would like to ask all of you to try to do something this year bigger and/or better than you did last year. And don't always do something and look for something in return. That's the real joy of giving!

## January 12, 2010

Today I went to Duke for my pulmonary test again. My FEV (forced expiratory volume) increased by eight. FEV is the maximum amount of air that I can forcefully exhale in one second. My DLCO (diffusing capacity of the lung for carbon monoxide) increased by thirteen. This is a measurement which shows how much oxygen is carried or transferred into the blood stream.

I guess it was good considering that it decreased when I was discharged from Duke. We will see on February third what all of this means.

## January 13, 2010

I had my appointment at the Gibson Cancer Center today. With all that I have gone through, my counts were within low normal ranges. There was some concern because my blood pressure was extremely high. When I was discharged from Duke, they told me that I did not have to continue taking my blood pressure pills. It was not and had not been an issue until now. However, the doctor reviewed my records from Duke and they said that if my blood pressure were to elevate again, that I would need to immediately take my blood pressure pills again. It was funny that the pharmacy had just called to my home a few days ago and said they had filled a prescription for me and it was ready to pick up. The thing is that the automated system does not tell you the name of the prescription. This is difficult when you have four and five medicines to keep up with. However, I found out later that the call was for my blood pressure pills.

Mommie and I went to the pharmacy to pick that up and then hit I-95 north to go home to Baltimore. We had to take care of business as it relates to Grandma.

We went to the cemetery and ordered a ceramic picture and a vase to be placed on her crypt. It is beautiful. It is fitting for the queen that she was. I cannot wait to see it when it comes. I guess that will be the next trip. We do have a few more trips to make. We are bringing things back gradually.

Daddy and I went to see Granddaddy William. He is in FutureCare also, as Grandma was. Ironically, he is in the exact same room as Grandma. Boy, it was hard being in that room. It was so surreal. There was one point that I could see Grandma lying in that same bed. Granddaddy William asked me why I had a sad look on my face. I told him that a thought of Grandma had just come across my mind for a moment. He knows that Grandma passed away, but I am not sure if he knows that Grandma was in this exact same room when she passed. Daddy remembered but we didn't say anything to Granddaddy William. He told me how Grandma was one of a kind. She truly was. Granddaddy William gave me a gift (door hanger) that he made in his Arts and Craft class.

That next day I was ready for the Ravens game. The Baltimore Ravens was going to play the Indianapolis Colts in the AFC Championship Playoff Game. Unfortunately, we lost. We left Sunday morning. Monday was a holiday, Dr. Martin Luther King, Jr.'s birthday. The boys were in Columbia, SC with my sister-in-law. There was no rush since school was out. They came back Monday afternoon. Michael had a dentist appointment later that day.

## *January 20, 2010*

I went to Gibson Cancer Center again on Wednesday. My report was good. My blood pressure, hemoglobin and white blood cell counts were much better. It was still low, but that is normal after having a transplant. She did not have my chemistry work yet. The nurse stated that if there was a problem, she would contact me. I never got a call that day so no news is good news. I will report again on next Wednesday.

## *January 24, 2010*

I went to my church, Oak Grove Missionary Baptist Church, today. I have not been since the Benefit Singing program the Missionary Department sponsored for me on October 4, 2009. It was really good to see everyone. Some I have seen here and there in public, but for the most part, I have not seen a majority of them. We had a wonderful time. It was fourth Sunday also. Fourth Sunday is Youth Sunday.

I really, really miss my young people. I take special interest in young people. I usually sit with them in the choir stand but I am still supposed to be avoiding crowds. I am sitting in the regular pews today. I am trying to be obedient! Boy, did they sing!

## *January 29, 2010*

Okay, yes, it has been a while since my last journal entry. Thanks to those who remind me that I need to keep everything all posted. I used to be good with this. I will do better. It's not like I'm doing anything else besides witting with my laptop.

I am going to the Gibson Cancer Center locally every Wednesday to get my blood drawn. They check my bloodwork and chemistry and all that good stuff. This past Wednesday, everything was exactly the same as last Wednesday. My counts are still low. But they said because I just had a bone marrow stem cell transplant, this is normal. So everything is good. I try to get out once a week. My mother has been making sure that I do alright. She is still here with me and I am so happy that she is.

Seems like I am always asking for something—please pray for my friend, Thomas Goode. You may have remembered me talking about a gentleman who was a few years younger than me who also had Multiple Myeloma. He had been coming to Duke once a month just for follow-up visits. He had been such an inspiration for me. I call him one of Duke's ambassadors. I mean he has been in brochures and everything. He is always so high spirited. Well, he just found out yesterday that his Myeloma has come back and come back in three different areas. It really has my heart a little saddened. Just say a prayer for him.

I cannot imagine what he is going through or what he is feeling. I mean, it is bad enough having the myeloma. Go through not one, but two transplants, only for it to come back a third time. I cannot see going through all of this again. But for the grace of God, have I made it through one and I am still not out of the woods yet.

My schedule for next week will be a little different. On Wednesday, I go to Duke to follow-up with the doctor there. On Thursday, I go back to Gibson Cancer Center and meet with my doctor there. They will then determine what schedule I will be on for my bloodwork.

I have also decided to participate in another clinical research study at Duke for fifteen months, something dealing with shingles. I'll give more information on my next update.

## *February 4, 2010*

I went to Duke on yesterday. Everything is okay. Well, it wasn't when I first went. Going back to square one—they took thirteen vials of blood from me. Thirteen!!! I told Marquita that I was good for five. She would not negotiate. I don't know what she saw funny. I was serious! Even though my weight has not changed (127 lbs), I told her that she has to leave me some blood.

Anyway, my levels are low, but that is normal since I have just had the transplant. Just record it and play it every time I come now. She said that it is very early. Maybe in three months, my counts should be going up. I am now in another clinical research trial because I recently underwent stem cell transplant for myeloma. People with decreased immunity due to disease or medical interventions (stem cell transplantation), have a higher risk of developing "shingles".

Herpes zoster, commonly known as "shingles", is a viral disease that is associated with infection by a virus called varicella-zoster virus.

It is characterized by a painful rash with blisters in a limited area on one side of the body or face, often appearing in a "belt-like" pattern.

The first sign of shingles is often pain or increased sensitivity in a specific area of the body, usually on only one side. Within a few days, a rash appears in the same area. The rash may begin as red spots. Shingles most often occurs on the trunk, but it can also occur on the face or limbs. The rash is usually painful and may also be itchy. Some people with shingles also have fever, muscle aches and headaches.

So, there is your biology lesson for the day. This is a fifteen month research trial. I will be required to get a vaccine shot once a month. On the day I get the shot and six days following, I must record my temperature, record any symptoms, muscle pain, tiredness, all of this good stuff. I have a dairy card that I must keep and turn in when I go the next month for the following vaccine. I get a new diary card and repeat the process.

So far, I am still sore in the arm from yesterday's shot. I'm glad they did it in the less dominant arm. I hope everyone is doing well. There is so much in the world going on. Just a side note, I saw my friend Thomas on yesterday and guess what—now on top of the myeloma possibly coming back, he has shingles. We did not get to talk much. We had to talk from a distance because shingles is contagious. He told me hello from the hallway as my blood was being drawn.

Be grateful for the little things in life!!! Grandma ALWAYS told me 'Don't complain because there is someone worse off than you who would love to trade places with you.' It makes me think about Thomas. He told me how he wished he would have been eligible to participate in the shingles clinical trial.

## *February 23, 2010*

It's been almost three weeks and I haven't posted anything. I know. I know. I did not post anything because I have not been to Duke nor the Gibson Cancer Center and I did not feel that there was a need to update. However, I have been admonished (I like that big word!) from several of you—that I should update to let you guys know how I am doing period. I did not want to make this thing boring. (I love my friends!)

I am doing well though. I have been to church the past three Sundays now. That was really against doctor's orders. You know, I am supposed to be avoiding crowds and stuff like that. They specified churches and schools on the top of their list. God will and has taken care of me thus far. It felt different being back up and doing the church announcements on yesterday. (I can never tell Ms. Mattie no) Boy, was I hurting in the afternoon though. We had our Male Choir Anniversary. I always video that program because Michael and Charles sing and Michael likes to watch those videos over and over again. The catch is where I position myself I must stand the entire time. I am not able to stand up for an extended amount of time and that was a two hour service. Boy, are my dogs barking!!! I was in some pain Sunday night and some yesterday but I tried not to stay on my feet too much yesterday. I'm a little better today. I thought I would have to call Duke.

As for my daily routine, I try to get outside at least once a day, if I don't go anywhere but to the grocery store or gas station and back. Some days I don't make it out though. I'm still having good days and bad days, but overall, I can't complain. My mom is still here with me. My dad still calls me every day sometimes two or three times a day. I love them both. I love all of you for somehow you have played a significant role in my life whether you know it or not. God places people in our lives for certain reasons and for certain seasons. Let me go and finish washing clothes. I had my CaringBridge family on my mind. I pray everyone is having a great day! Love you all!

## *March 3, 2010*

Today was my second vaccination for my shingles. I had an eleven o'clock appointment at Duke. Boy, were we pushing it since the kids had a two hour delay. And for what? A chance of ice? It kills me how they always have a two hour delay here and nothing happens. No snow. No ice. I know—better safe than sorry. It just makes me think of the days when I had to go to school with snow up to my knees. I guess that's the difference between being raised in the city versus the country.

But still made it at 10:57. I weighed in at 129 lbs. Blood pressure was good—113/75. I gave them six vials of blood. Got my second shingles shot. Got my new diary card. Now, I'll hurt for the next five or six days. They said I look good at Duke. I don't feel it. I'm definitely not at full capacity. I'm getting there though. I had two bad days last week. I do not feel like I am connected with Grandma like I was when she was living. But I over did it a little. I know I did. I thought in my "Superwoman" mode for a moment. Mommie was really upset. I believe that Mommie got Grandma to come to me and tell me to slow down. Mommie knows that when I don't listen to anyone, I will listen to Macie Barber. I could hear Grandma fussing at me as if she were right in front of me. It worked. So, I go to Gibson Cancer Center on March fifteenth. I go back to Duke on April first. Until then, everyone be blessed!

## *March 10, 2010*

I forgot to mention in my prior journal entry that I had an appointment with my primary care physician, Dr. Shetty. That was yesterday. She stated the last time that I saw her that she wanted to see me every six months. She said that she knew I was in good hands with Duke and they would take care of me. All I can say is that she did my vitals and all of that was good. She was concerned as to why I was back on the blood pressure pills and I told her that story. She said I looked very good after just having a transplant. And that was that. I really did not see the need to go. I was close to calling and canceling and saving my thirty dollars copay, . . . but I was obedient.

I was happy to see some familiar faces at the doctor's office also. I was happy to see Ms. Mae Love, a very special woman to me. :) I also saw Mr. Bill and Mrs. Sue Prevatte. It has been a long time since I saw them. Was very glad to see everyone. Things are okay. Hope everyone is doing well and I will check in with you on next week after I see Dr. Ahmed at the Gibson Cancer Center.

## *March 16, 2010*

Yesterday was my appointment with Dr. Ahmed at the Gibson Cancer Center in Lumberton. Everything is the same. I do not have my exact count numbers. If something were wrong, they would not have let me out so everything must be good. No news is good news.

I have had a very disturbing, bothersome, constant dry cough. She prescribed me some generic Zyrtec. So, we will see how that pans out. Dr. Ahmed then asked me about coming to this cancer support group. They meet once a month. I think this will be good. So many people have helped and encouraged me along the way. This will be my chance to give back.

To my bald Caucasian brother, Paul (I bet everyone wonders why I single him out so much. I love him like that ☺) I pick with him worse at work! You know, I was rocking the bald thing for a minute and like Mr. Gentry said, hey, there is minimal work to it. I had practically convinced myself that I could do this. I just needed more headbands to match more of my outfits. But now, . . . now, my hair is trying to come back, people! I have to wash it every day and take care of it. That is work. I never liked doing my hair when it was long. Which do you like? Long hair or short hair? Maybe one day, I'll take a before picture and an after picture and let you guys vote and decide. Then we will see what everyone decides at the end of this six month recovery. Just a thought.

I do not see Dr. Ahmed for another six weeks (April twenty-seventh). I go back to Duke on April first. That will be a long day. I have to have another pulmonary function (breathing) test early that morning. See Dr. G for my three month follow-up, do the bloodwork and get my third shingles shot for the month.

Coughed most of the night and woke up late this morning. I got these boys (Michael and Jimarius) running around the house like crazy so they do not miss the bus. I must have dozed off hard because I do not remember CJ leaving. That was usually my cue to wake up. So, that's why I am up so early, in case you ask. Got a load of clothes washing. Might as well stay up and watch the news. This is killing me—not being able to work. If I had some hair, boy, I would be pulling it out right now. I am trying to keep myself busy without over doing it and without having Grandma leave Heaven to come pay me a visit and fuss me out, as before.

## *March 30, 2010*

My heart is really heavy today. I just wanted to ask everyone to pray for my sister, my best friend, my ride-or-die girl, Venita Walker.

Her father passed away today. I want to be with her so bad. I feel the need to be with her because she has always been and continues to be there for me, no matter what. Pray for traveling mercies for her and her family as they travel from Charlotte to New York. Me? Doing okay. Had some episodes but I'm alright—just worried about my sister.

## *April 1, 2010*

Today was my visit at Duke. Got there an hour early (ten thirty am). Had bloodwork done to get that out of the way. They took twelve vials of blood. Weight still maintaining at 127 and vitals are looking good. I was then shuttled to the clinic to the pulmonary function department for my pulmonary function (breathing) test.

After several (and I mean, several) rounds of tests, I increased three percent in one thing and five percent in the other. Remember when I gave you guys that class on DLCO and the other thing? [It's late. I can't remember right now.] As Mommie and I were walking back to the front of the clinic, I was reading my report not looking where I was walking and who walks right in front of me on purpose? . . . my friend, Thomas.

It was really good to see him. I had not seen him since he caught the shingles and he was isolated then. Thomas, Mommie and myself had a good time coming back on the shuttle. We both had appointments with Dr. G. I did not know that I did not have my third shingles shot. I get two shots and the third visit, there is no shot. They want to see how I am doing. Then they will start with the shots again. I did get my diary card as before where I will have to keep up with any fever and stuff like that. Believe it or not, I was ready for the shot.

They are concerned that my white blood count is very low again. I had two episodes of throwing up. One happened two days ago and the other last week. They are saying that it may be very low because in the course of throwing up, my body may have had to fight off some infection associated with the throwing up. But if this is not the case, this is a big concern. {Okay, not a repeat situation, . . . I refuse to believe it.} So, they want me to get bloodwork drawn again next week and see where my counts are then.

Did not think about it at that time—but we are leaving to go home (Baltimore) since the boys are out of school for spring break.

We were going to be gone all next week. I will have to call tomorrow and see if I can get it done Friday and I guess we will leave for Baltimore on Thursday.

I have also been experiencing a really bad stiffness in my joints every time I get up and walk after lying down or sitting for an extended period of time. I know that they discussed a bone strengthener earlier in this process. I was thinking that this was a pill or something to take. No, it is an IV you take once a month. Uggghhhh!!!! I asked them if they had it in a liquid. They laughed and said no. I was serious!!! They looked in my file and according to my bone survey, I do not need it. Well, why in the heck am I feeling like this? I hurt so bad. Well, they broke down the news and told me that I have, . . . get this . . . arthritis. No one ever told me to look forward to these things at forty.

I go back to Duke April twenty-ninth (fourth shingles shot) and July first (three month doctor visit). So, that's about it. Enjoy the nice weather and the break. Remember Easter is not about the chocolate bunnies and new clothes, but about Jesus being resurrected to save us from ourselves.

## *April 3, 2010*

Well, we (me, Mommie, CJ, Michael and CJ's best friend [I call him my adopted son], Eugene) made it home to Baltimore. We left Lumberton about three fifteen am and arrived in Baltimore at nine thirty am. We were home maybe an hour when Edie called. She came over and we all went to the movies to see 'Clash of the Titans'. It was a pretty good movie. Greek mythology and all that stuff.

During that hour of waiting, my cousin from two houses next door came. This was a shocker for her. She is one of the many family members who still did not know about my cancer. She came over and saw me with my head wrap off. She definitely questioned why my hair was nearly gone. We went back and forth. I really meant to tell her but I just did not. We got on the subject of my aunt (Grandma's sister) who is having some physical health issues so the discussion about me got diverted. That was great.

Then I took Mommie to the grocery store to get some stuff for the week. Then had another hour break and Daddy picked up me and the boys and took us to *Dave and Buster's*.

I guess CJ outgrew Dave and Buster's. I did not think anyone could outgrow it. After we all ate in the food court, CJ and Eugene did what normal teenage boys do—walk the mall. So, Daddy, Michael and myself enjoyed D&B for the next four or five hours. Boy, was I beat when I got home. I took a shower and went to bed. I did not even stay awake enough to take my evening medicine. I fell asleep watching 'The Ten Commandments'. A good time was had by all. That was what was important. Family time. The little things.

All I could think about was a preacher Mommie and I listened to as we were driving from DC into Maryland. Her message was taken from the eleventh chapter of Mark. Her message was 'God has a plan for you.' All day and all night, this message has struck home with me. The past year just went through my mind in a matter of twenty-five minutes.

God does have a plan for each and every one of us. This is Easter time, where we celebrate the resurrection of our Lord and Savior Jesus Christ. One thing I learned is that a donkey is a cross between a horse and a mule. I didn't know that. Her point was that Jesus even had a plan for the donkey. He being who He is, could have rode on a stallion, but He chose a donkey. There was a plan for that donkey. If God has a plan for a donkey, surely he has a plan for every one of us. If you put your hand over your heart and you feel your heart beating that means that God has a plan for you and has given you another opportunity to do right and to do His will to fulfill His plan. "For I know the plans I have for you", declares the Lord, "plans to prosper you and not to harm you, plans to give you hope and a future." Jeremiah 29:11.

I have always believed that, but it really hit home listening to her. I have always believed that if you are still alive, it is because there is a plan that He has to have fulfilled. And His plan IS going to be fulfilled. I feel that when people pass, God's will for that person's life has been completed.

## *April 4, 2010*

Today is Easter Sunday. I did not go to church. It felt awkward. I guess because this is the first Easter without Grandma. I just was not ready to go. I have no explanation. We were invited to Edie's house for Sunday dinner. We had fun until . . . it was time to eat. I ate some delicious greens, and some tasty macaroni and cheese, and then I had two deviled eggs. After I had that second deviled egg, . . . that is when I remembered that I cannot eat eggs. Since the transplant, my body rejects certain foods to include eggs, bananas [after all that I have swallowed during this process], syrup and sweet potato pie—that we know of now. My head was in Edie's commode throwing up again. I was alright after that. At least, I did get to taste the eggs. I love deviled eggs. We watched several movies and took some pictures. We left about eight thirty that evening. Today was a good day.

## *April 5, 2010*

Today we went to see Aunt Lou. Aunt Lou is Charles' aunt who resides in Baltimore. Every time we are home, we always visit her. Her husband, Uncle Raymond, passed away in June which is when I was diagnosed with cancer and I was unable to attend the funeral. She called when Grandma passed away and I was in the shower. I did not get to call her back. There was so much going on. Her health had been going down as well so I really felt the need to see her. We took pictures and enjoyed our time with her.

Next, the boys and I went to see my godmother who does not live far from Aunt Lou. One thing she made me promise at Grandma's funeral is that we would never forget her. I promised her that. I wanted to call but I said it would not be a surprise then. We drove over there and she was walking up her stairway from pulling weeds outside. I drove up beside her and rolled down the window. She was so surprised. She nearly cried. She feed us some pork chops, rice and greens. Eugene and Michael tried to act shy. Nothing shy about CJ and myself. She was still the same. There has never been a time my whole life when you did not go over there and she did not feed you. We took pictures there also. I believe that pictures are worth a thousand words. They can hold so many memories.

We left there and met Daddy at the bowling alley. Grandma was an avid bowler. She was a faithful league member for years, I mean since I was little. We had fun bowling and eating pizza. These past two days have been non-stop. Gotta enjoy it. Quality family time. That's what up!

## *April 6, 2010*

We have been going non-stop since we have been here. Today is a relaxed day. Mommie wanted to go to BestBuy to find a CD and Michael had some money that was just burning his pockets. He wanted to buy a game for his PlayStation2. So, we went to BestBuy and then went to the mall. When we came back, I spent time with my aunt. All I can say in my mind is she looks just like Grandma. Why wouldn't she? That's her sister.

Daddy called asking if I or the boys wanted to do anything. As we talked about it, there was nothing left to do. We have done every thing. Daddy needed some rest anyway. Everyone was going back to work now. They were not on break like us. I told him that I wanted to see Granddaddy William. Daddy was very against it saying that there are too many germs floating around the nursing home and he totally advised against it. I told him that I would wear a mask. That did not matter to him. I guess I will just have to call him. I also need to call my daddy's sister.

Got a call from Charles that one of our church mothers just passed away. We are very close to their entire family. It was surprising to me to learn that she had Multiple Myeloma years and years and years ago. I learned about this from her daughter, who was a great comfort to me when I received my diagnosis. She had been sick for some time and had other issues going on. The wake is Friday and the funeral is Saturday. Well, we are leaving on Thursday so I will do all I can to make the funeral. The daughter wanted me to be the Mistress of Ceremonies for the wake. Wow, I had never heard of such. She is also one I can never say no to.

## *April 16, 2010*

Happy birthday to me, Happy birthday to me, Happy birthday to meeee, Happy birthday to me! Thank you Lord for letting me see fourty-one years of life. I already miss my Grandma mailing me a birthday card. She was always the first to call early in the morning to sing happy birthday to me. God, I miss her!

## *April 23, 2010*

Well, today and tomorrow is the American Cancer Society's Relay for Life at Lumberton Senior High School. I had always heard about this annual event. I did not really know or understand it . . . until now. Relay for Life is "a life-changing event that gives everyone in communities across the globe a chance to celebrate the lives of people who have battled cancer, remember loved ones lost, and fight back against the disease."

There are three components—Celebrate (The Survivors Lap), Remember (The Luminaria Ceremony) and the Fight Back Ceremony. If you get a chance, check out their website at www.relayforlife.org. I had been asked by several people if I was going to participate. If I were feeling more physically able, I would have. When I have a passion for something, I really put my all into it.

I'm sure in your life, you know at least one person (if not more) who is or was battling cancer. I would like to ask that you just take a brief second and just say a prayer of comfort for that individual and their caregiver(s) and their family. I promise you that if you do that, you too will be comforted.

Have a blessed night! (Mia Chavis—words cannot express how I feel about you doing the luminaria in my honor tonight! I love ya, girl!)

## *April 27, 2010*

I had my appointment today at the Gibson Cancer Center. Vitals were okay. During a physical exam, Dr. Ahmed noticed that my thyroid on my right side is swollen. I have to go for an ultrasound on Friday. They said this could come from a cyst, a tumor or just hyper activity.

She is also going to call Dr. Gasperetto at Duke to see why I am not on Zometa. Zometa is an IV medicine that is somewhat like a bone strengthener. I'll have to check the status of that on Friday also. Been on the tired side today, along with what seemed to be an oncoming migraine.

Go to Duke on Thursday. Get the ultrasound on Friday at the local hospital. Was sick the weekend. Found out that I can add one more item to the list (of foods that my body is rejecting). Why are all of them my favorite foods so far—eggs, syrup, bananas and on Sunday, macaroni and cheese. You know, I think about all of the bananas they tried to shove down my throat during treatment, . . . I guess I would reject it too. :) All in all, I'm good. I won't complain!

## *April 30, 2010*

Well, I went to Duke on yesterday for my shingles shot—the worse! Your arm is soar for six days. I have to keep up with the diary card recording my temperature everyday and if the area is red, swollen, etc. Today I am in so much pain. My temp was 101.5. I've been having hot and cold flashes. I have a headache that won't quit. Didn't feel like getting up to go to the hospital for the ultrasound, but we did. Guess I'll have to wait to hear from the doctor about the results.

CTE Family—you guys are da bomb! I really enjoyed being with you all for lunch last Tuesday and this past Wednesday at the Career Exploration Fair. I love and miss all of you!!!

## *May 9, 2010*

HAPPY MOTHER'S DAY! (Sorry that the day is about over and I am just getting a chance to wish all the ladies a Happy Mother's Day). Have not had computer access for a couple of days since I have been out of town.

First, let me say that I totally forgot to update everyone with last Friday's ultrasound results. Different people were asking me and I said 'Oh, I did not put it on the website'. Anyway, the results were negative. They did not see anything as we knew they would.

Both doctors are still going back and forth about the Zometa medicine (bone medicine). My Duke doctor told my Duke doctor here in Lumberton (just as she told me earlier when I asked her) that according to my bone survey and bone scan, I do not need it. My local Duke doctor is saying that if I wanted to use it that I could. I'm praying about that and see where the Lord leads. My bones are really hurting though.

Had a busy weekend. Saturday morning Michael had baseball practice. We then headed to Charlotte and spent the rest of the day and night with my sister. Got up Sunday morning and headed to Rock Hill, SC and went to church with Mom. They were honoring her and she didn't know it. I kept wondering how they were keeping it from her. I talked to her Saturday and she was at church doing the bulletins. Come to find out today that she did the programs, but hers did not have the front page with her picture and a write-up and the write-up we did for her.

Boy, was she shocked! She balled like a baby. Guess that's where I get it from. :) I began to cry only because I wish Grandma could have been there. This was a rough Mother's Day. It's the first without Grandma. I had my moment on Friday and just boo-hooed to myself.

Pictures are worth a thousand words. I love taking pictures and I love being taken. I looked at the pictures in my digital camera and saw all the pictures from last Mother's Day when we spent time with Grandma. She was at Frederick Villa then. I never thought then that it would be our last Mother's Day with her.

Treasure every moment with those you love! Make sure that people know that you love them. You never know when it will be your last.

## *June 4, 2010*

Went to Duke on Wednesday. It was visit five for my clinical trial study for the shingles. No shot today. Just had to turn in my diary card for the month where I record my temperature, and note any fevers or irregularities, stuff like that. Visit six will be in March 2011 which will end the fifteen month clinical trial. From now until then, they will call me once a month to check on my status. They drew tons of blood from me. I didn't believe that they left me any, but they assured me that they did.

Let's see—since I last talked with you, I have had two deaths in the family—Charles' cousin in Lumberton and a cousin of mine in Columbia, SC. I was happy to see everyone at the funeral and then kind of nervous at the same time. This was a cousin on Grandma's side of the family. Many still do not know of my condition. I agreed with my cousin, Kristina, who hugged me and said that we have to stop meeting like this. (The last time I saw her [or any of them] was at Grandma's funeral). Some were missing the long hair, [I did not go into explanation] but they like the short do. ***There's nothing like family!***

Just when I want to tell them, I get a call this past Monday from my cousin who is in the hospital at home (Baltimore) with pneumonia. This is the brother of the cousin who just passed. I tell you when it rains, it storms! We have a family reunion July fifteenth through eighteenth, so *maybe* I will tell them then.

I am so looking forward to going back to work. Last day of school for the students is next Thursday. Everyone is happy to get out and I'm ready to gooooo! Those who know me know that I have been extremely good to be at home all this time. [Gimme a hand clap! Yes, thank you very much!] But the time has come now—I am so ready to go back to work. I miss my students so bad! Just don't know what school I will be at when I return??? (Anybody know?)

## *June 17, 2010*

Good afternoon CaringBridge Family,

Well, . . . it has been exactly a year to the hour that I was at Duke University Medical Center. Charles and I were in Dr. Frederick Diehl's office. He gave me a pathology report and officially diagnosed me with cancer. I sat up last night and reflected on a year ago. Preparing for the drive up. Praying for Charles in preparation of the news for him. Wondering how I was going to tell my two "men" (and I never even got to tell them). Hearing the words that I would probably have five years to live. Praying that I just have to see my two boys graduate and become successful citizens in society. Thinking how those three words (You have cancer) would change the rest of my life.

I had not really reflected on this so heavily until last night. I think how the matriarch of my family, my grandmother, passed away. (That's been far worse to deal with compared to the cancer) And since then, I have had six deaths. Seems like a death every month. I have never been surrounded by so much death.

However, my faith has grown so tremendously until you could not believe. We are going to Vacation Bible School at a neighboring church, not our home church. The topic is "Hero Headquarters." The title of the adult handbook is UNNAMED. The subtopics include

UNWORTHY, UNEXPECTED, UNNOTICED, UNPOLISHED, UNDERESTIMATED, UNCERTAIN and UNRANKED. Yesterday we discussed UNWORTHY.

I can remember telling everyone last year how I put God up against a wall and said "Why me?" and he replied "Why not you?" He told me that He was going to perform a work in me that I could not even understand, even if He outlined it in black and white. All I could think to myself is "what good can come out of something so bad?" (UNEXPECTED).

I cannot begin to tell you all of the good that has come about within the past year. If I told you individually, YOU would not believe. I feel like the unnamed Roman officer at Capernaum who told God that he is UNWORTHY but he told God that if He would just speak the word that his servant would be healed. Sometimes in our life, all God has to do is SPEAK the word.

As I explained to them yesterday, sometimes we ask for things from God but it comes to us in a package that we least expect. I am so thankful to all of my family and friends for hanging in there on this journey. Granted, everything is not over, but we are taking one day at a time. I may not have gotten a chance to email or call everyone who has posted on my guestbook, but you have all played a remarkable role in this journey.

You have made the journey worth while! Have a great evening and a great summer to all of my educational colleagues!!! I miss you guys a bunch!!! I hope to see you all next school year!

## TO BE CONTINUED . . . .

Well, there is no ending to this conclusion. Today is August 18, 2012 and all is well. It has been three years. Of course, I have to put some type of transitional ending to this or otherwise, I am writing this book forever. I still have some bad days, but I have some good ones too. As I write this, I have just come back home from sending my oldest son to East Carolina University. I am so proud of him. He graduated third in his class. He plans to major in Exercise Physiology. I wish so much that Grandma were alive to see this day. I know that she was with us in spirit.

I can remember when I told my sista that I was gonna make it through this and that I prayed that the Lord would let me see both of my boys graduate from high school. Well, here is one whom he let me see graduate. I have five more years for the other. (God help me!)

My concluding message is this: No matter what you are going through, you must keep your head up and finish the fight. Everybody is going through something. Some people may not want to admit it. Your situation may be different from mine, but we are all going through a trial of some sort. God is preparing you for something so much bigger and better. Unless you complete the course before you, you will never make it to the next level.

The devil may try to tell you to quit and give up. That it is not worth it. He distracts you and tries to persuade you to throw in the towel. Do not discount what you are going through. God is using it all to prepare you for the anointing that he is putting on you. You have to have this test completed and under your belt to get you ready for the next level.

I do not know where I would be today if I had given up. If I decided to not take the medicines or if I decided to not take the chemo, . . . I do not know if I would have seen my oldest son's graduation. I do not know if I would have been able to write and encourage someone. Who knows if I would even have been alive? I did not write this book to be a number one seller. I wrote this book to inspire someone who may have been diagnosed with Multiple Myeloma and to let you know that you can make it. You got to trust and have faith in God. Yeah, it is easier said than done. Nobody knows that better than me. You cannot always go by how things look on the outside. You must finish the task set before you and you will be amazed at what God will have in store for you.

# Favorite Quotest that Helped Me Get Through

- ➤ Find out who you are—not only in good times, but when you are strong.
- ➤ Life isn't about waiting for the storm to pass; it's about learning to dance in the rain.
- ➤ Anyone can give up; it's the easiest thing in the world to do. But to hold it together when everyone else would understand if you fell apart, that's true strength.
- ➤ People might not get all they work for in this world, but they must certainty work for all they get—Frederick Douglass
- ➤ Enjoy when you can, and endure when you must.—Johann Wolfgang von Goethe

# ENDNOTES

[1] Merriam-Webster Online Dictionary, www.merriam-webster.com/dictionary/chemotheraphy, Accessed January 28, 2010.

[2] WebMD Medical Reference from Healthwise, "Vancomycin-Resistant Enterococci (VRE) Overview", http://www.webmd.com/a-to-z-guides/vancomycin-resistant-enterococci-vre-overview Accessed July 5, 2012.

[3] Blood Bank: Irradiation, http://bloodbank-egypt.com/Irradiation.htm Accessed July 7, 2012.

[4] Medical Encyclopedia, Reasons for a D and C, January 21, 2009, http://ehealthforum.com/health/reasons_for_d_and_c-e17.html, Accessed January 14, 2010.